TRACING YOUR INSOLVENT ANCESTORS

FAMILY HISTORY FROM PEN & SWORD

Tracing Secret Service Ancestors
•
Tracing Your Air Force Ancestors
•
Tracing Your Ancestors
•
Tracing Your Ancestors from 1066 to 1837
•
Tracing Your Ancestors Through Death Records
•
Tracing Your Ancestors Through Family Photographs
•
Tracing Your Ancestors Using the Census
•
Tracing Your Ancestors' Childhood
•
Tracing Your Ancestors' Parish Records
•
Tracing Your Aristocratic Ancestors
•
Tracing Your Army Ancestors – 2nd Edition
•
Tracing Your Birmingham Ancestors
•
Tracing Your Black Country Ancestors
•
Tracing Your British Indian Ancestors
•
Tracing Your Canal Ancestors
•
Tracing Your Channel Islands Ancestors
•
Tracing Your Coalmining Ancestors
•
Tracing Your Criminal Ancestors
•
Tracing Your East Anglian Ancestors
•
Tracing Your East End Ancestors
•
Tracing Your Edinburgh Ancestors
•
Tracing Your First World War Ancestors
•
Tracing Your Great War Ancestors: The Gallipoli Campaign
•
Tracing Your Great War Ancestors: The Somme
•
Tracing Your Great War Ancestors: Ypres
•
Tracing Your Huguenot Ancestors
•
Tracing Your Jewish Ancestors

Tracing Your Labour Movement Ancestors
•
Tracing Your Lancashire Ancestors
•
Tracing Your Leeds Ancestors
•
Tracing Your Legal Ancestors
•
Tracing Your Liverpool Ancestors
•
Tracing Your London Ancestors
•
Tracing Your Medical Ancestors
•
Tracing Your Merchant Navy Ancestors
•
Tracing Your Naval Ancestors
•
Tracing Your Northern Ancestors
•
Tracing Your Pauper Ancestors
•
Tracing Your Police Ancestors
•
Tracing Your Prisoner of War Ancestors: The First World War
•
Tracing Your Railway Ancestors
•
Tracing Your Royal Marine Ancestors
•
Tracing Your Rural Ancestors
•
Tracing Your Scottish Ancestors
•
Tracing Your Second World War Ancestors
•
Tracing Your Servant Ancestors
•
Tracing Your Service Women Ancestors
•
Tracing Your Shipbuilding Ancestors
•
Tracing Your Tank Ancestors
•
Tracing Your Textile Ancestors
•
Tracing Your Trade and Craftsmen Ancestors
•
Tracing Your Welsh Ancestors
•
Tracing Your West Country Ancestors
•
Tracing Your Yorkshire Ancestors

TRACING YOUR INSOLVENT ANCESTORS

A Guide for Family and Local Historians

Paul Blake

Pen & Sword
FAMILY HISTORY

First published in Great Britain in 2019
PEN & SWORD FAMILY HISTORY
an imprint of
Pen & Sword Books Ltd
47 Church Street, Barnsley, South Yorkshire, S70 2AS

Copyright © Paul Blake, 2019

ISBN 978 1 52673 865 3

The right of Paul Blake to be identified as Author
of the Work has been asserted by him in accordance
with the Copyright, Designs and Patents Act 1988.

A CIP catalogue record for this book is
available from the British Library.

All rights reserved. No part of this book may be reproduced or
transmitted in any form or by any means, electronic or mechanical
including photocopying, recording or by any information storage
and retrieval system, without permission from the Publisher in writing.

Typeset in Palatino and Optima by CHIC GRAPHICS

Printed and bound in England by TJ International Ltd, Padstow, Cornwall

Pen & Sword Books Ltd incorporates the imprints of Pen & Sword
Airworld, Archaeology, Atlas, Aviation, Battleground, Discovery, Family
History, Fiction, History, Maritime, Military, Military Classics, Politics,
Select, Social History, True Crime, Frontline Books, Leo Cooper,
Remember When, Seaforth Publishing, The Praetorian Press,
Wharncliffe Local History, Wharncliffe Transport,
Wharncliffe True Crime and White Owl.

For a complete list of Pen & Sword titles please contact

PEN & SWORD BOOKS LTD
47 Church Street, Barnsley, South Yorkshire, S70 2AS, England
E-mail: enquiries@pen-and-sword.co.uk
Website: www.pen-and-sword.co.uk
or
PEN & SWORD BOOKS LTD
1950 Lawrence Rd., Havertown, PA 19083, USA
E-mail: Uspen-and-sword@casematepublishers.com
Website: www.penandswordbooks.com

CONTENTS

Preface		ix
Chapter 1	Insolvent Debtors – Background	1
	Exposing Defaulters	5
Chapter 2	The Machinery of Justice	9
	The Courts	12
	Common Law Courts	13
	Court of Common Pleas	15
	Court of King's (or Queen's) Bench	16
	Exchequer of Pleas (or Court of Exchequer)	17
	Equity Courts	18
	Chancery Court	18
	Court of Requests	18
	Court of Star Chamber	19
	Palace Court	19
	Assize Courts	19
	Palatinate of Lancaster Court of Common Pleas	20
	Supreme Court of Judicature	20
Chapter 3	Relief and Release	21
	Charity	23
	Court for Relief of Insolvent Debtors	25
Chapter 4	Insolvent Debtors – Courts and Court Records	30
	Common Law Courts	32
	Court of Common Pleas	32
	Court of King's (or Queen's) Bench	39
	Exchequer of Pleas (or Court of Exchequer)	44
	John Doe and Richard Roe	48

	Equity Courts	49
	Court of Requests	49
	Court of Star Chamber	51
	Palace Court	52
	Palatinate of Lancaster Court of Common Pleas	55
Chapter 5	Insolvent Debtors – Imprisonment	58
Chapter 6	Insolvent Debtors – Common Law and Central Prisons and Prison Records	65
	The Gordon Riots	70
	Fleet Prison	72
	Fleet Marriages	77
	Marshalsea Prison	80
	King's (Queen's) Bench Prison and Queen's Prison	83
	Whitecross Street Prison	87
	Horsemonger Lane Prison	90
	Newgate Prison	92
	Records	92
	Fleet Prison	93
	Marshalsea Prison	99
	King's (Queen's) Bench Prison	101
	Whitecross Street Prison	106
	Horsemonger Lane Prison	108
	Newgate Prison	108
	Other Prison Records	109
	Census Returns	111
Chapter 7	Insolvent Debtors – London Courts and Court Records	113
	City of London Courts	114
	Mayor's Court	115
	Sheriffs' Court	117
	City of London Court	120
	Court of Requests	121
	Court of Requests for the City of London	123

	County Courts	124
	Sanctuary	125
Chapter 8	**Insolvent Debtors – London Prisons and Records**	132
	London Compters	132
	Poultry Compter	132
	Wood Street Compter	134
	Giltspur Street Compter	137
	Southwark Compter	139
	Whitechapel Prison	141
	Ludgate Prison	142
	Prisoners' Inquests	142
	Release of Insolvent Debtors in the City of London	142
	Release of Insolvent Debtors in Middlesex	145
	Release of Insolvent Debtors in Southwark	146
Chapter 9	**County Debtors**	150
	Find-an-archive	150
	Trial	152
	Quarter Sessions	152
	Court of Requests	152
	County Courts	153
	Prisons	153
	Reports of the Inspectors of Prisons of Great Britain	154
	Records Examples	157
	Wiltshire	157
	Dorset	161
	Surrey	162
Chapter 10	**Bankruptcy**	165
	Courts of Bankruptcy	171
	Records	172
	Bankruptcy Case Files	173

	Bankruptcy Proceedings before 1869	177
	Bankruptcy Proceedings from 1869	180
	Bankruptcy Appeals	182
	Bankruptcy Functions of the Board of Trade	183
	Oscar Wilde	185
Chapter 11	**Newspapers, Periodicals, Journals and Directories**	187
	Newspapers, Periodicals and Journals	187
	Directories	195
Appendix A: Acts of Parliament		198
Appendix B: Regnal Years		207
Useful Addresses and Websites		209
Bibliography		211
List of Illustrations		214
Index		218

PREFACE

Debt is nothing new; it is not a phenomenon of recent centuries. Debt, leading to insolvency and bankruptcy, was not a rare occurrence in the lives of our ancestors: many, perhaps most, lived on credit. Until relatively recent times, although they may not have committed any criminal offence, debtors and bankrupts were perceived to be evasive at best and fraudulent at worst. Over the centuries, debt and bankruptcy have had an enormous impact on the lives of ordinary individuals and families, whose only crime may have been misfortune.

As Charles Dickens's Mr Micawber famously observed:

> Annual income twenty pounds, annual expenditure nineteen pounds nineteen and six, result happiness. Annual income twenty pounds, annual expenditure twenty pounds ought and six, result misery.

Mr Micawber, who appeared in Dickens's eighth novel *David Copperfield*, is said to have been based on Dickens's own father who, like the character, was incarcerated in a debtors' prison.

Regulations relating to bankruptcy appear as part of just about every legal system and are found as far back as 2250 BCE in the Hammurabi Code. In Roman times and in medieval Europe, debtors were liable to have their property seized and handed over to creditors. Ancient laws used a variety of methods for distributing losses among creditors, and satisfaction for the creditor usually came from the debtor's own bodily expense. He might be imprisoned, enslaved or killed, or even all three. In England, the Magna Carta Liberatum in 1215 set out rules that a person's land could not be seized if they had chattels or money sufficient to repay their creditors.

The Statute of Merchants in 1285 made it possible for creditors to register major debts and use imprisonment to enforce them. In 1351 the use of immediate imprisonment was extended to civil debt in general. This introduced a practice that would cause appalling misery for centuries to come. It was now possible for a creditor to obtain a warrant from the courts, which were then allowed to gaol anyone who had not paid for goods they had received. There he, or she, would stay indefinitely, pending satisfaction by their creditor.

Commitment to prison did not in itself extinguish the debt. The purpose of this seemingly extreme measure was to force people who could pay to do so, the threat of imprisonment being sufficient leverage for them to raise the money somehow and settle the debt without any further delay.

Numerous Acts of Parliament between 1670 and 1800 introduced procedures that allowed for the release of insolvent debtors from prison by applying to Justices of the Peace. In 1813 a Court for the Relief of Insolvent Debtors was established.

Nevertheless, even in the nineteenth century the rules surrounding bankruptcy and debt were complex. There was always a clear distinction between debt and bankruptcy – the insolvent debtor and the bankrupt – and it is important to understand the difference between the two. Until 1842, the legal status of being a bankrupt, and therefore able to pay off creditors and be discharged of all outstanding debts, was confined to traders owing more than £100 – the emphasis being on 'trader'.

Debtors who were not traders – which by the eighteenth century included most skilled craftsmen – did not qualify to become bankrupt, but were given the status of 'insolvent debtor'. Notably, farmers were specifically excluded from this regulation. Those debtors who were not eligible to claim bankruptcy remained insolvent, subject to common law, and, if their creditors wished, were confined indefinitely in prison, responsible for their debts but

Preface

unable to pay them. They were frequently held in the same prisons as convicted criminal offenders or those remanded for trial, and often formed one of the largest groups of prisoners. Not until 1861 were insolvent debtors allowed to apply for bankruptcy.

The Insolvent Debtors Act 1842 allowed non-traders to begin bankruptcy proceedings for relief from debts. Any person not being a trader, or being a trader and owing less than £300, could obtain a protection order from the Court of Bankruptcy or a District Court of Bankruptcy staying all process against them on condition of vesting all their property in an official assignee.

The 1861 Bankruptcy Act abolished the Court for the Relief of Insolvent Debtors and transferred its jurisdiction to the Bankruptcy Court. It authorized registrars of the Court of Bankruptcy to visit prisons and adjudge bankrupt those imprisoned for debt who satisfied them as to the genuineness of their insolvency. This resulted in a dramatic fall in the number of debtors in prison.

Some debtors were imprisoned through no fault of their own: the Bedford gaoler in 1858 complained that 73 out of the 122 debtors sent to the gaol owed money to hawkers (door-to-door salesmen) who had left goods with them, without being asked to do so, who then took them to court when they would not or could not pay.

As far back as 1650, William Leach estimated that there were 20,000 debtors in gaol. It is probable that in London and other major towns as many were incarcerated for debt as for crime. During the eighteenth and early nineteenth century, more than half of all prisoners were debtors, with some 10,000 people being imprisoned for debt each year. In 1777, John Howard found that 2,437 out of a total of 4,084 inmates were imprisoned for debt. More than 30,000 debtors were arrested in England in 1837.

Although debtors were imprisoned throughout the country, London was infamous for its debtors' prisons. The Fleet is probably the best known, but there were several others: Coldbath Fields Prison, Giltspur Street Compter, the King's Bench Prison, the Marshalsea Prison, Poultry Compter and Wood Street Compter. It was in the Marshalsea that John Dickens, the author's father, was imprisoned. As a consequence, debtors' prisons feature in several of Dickens's novels: Mr Pickwick was sent to the Fleet and Mr Micawber was imprisoned in the King's Bench. Most famously, Little Dorrit's father spent much of his life in the Marshalsea.

In some towns and cities beyond London, there were also separate prisons for debtors, but in most cases the debtors were simply kept apart from other prisoners in their own wings. Conditions overall were better than in the main prison. Debtors did not have to do hard labour. They were allowed extensive privileges compared with other prisoners, including being allowed visitors, their own food and clothing, and the right to work at their trade or profession as far as was possible while remaining imprisoned. The small amounts that they could earn were usually not sufficient to cover their keep. Sometimes prison rules were applied loosely: in 1814 the gaoler in Bedford admitted that he had used a debtor as a 'turnkey' (prison guard) for which, along with other offences, he was sacked.

In the early eighteenth century, a committee of MPs led by Sir James Oglethorpe investigated conditions in the debtors' prisons. They found evidence of physical abuse and torture (including the use of thumbscrews) along with appalling overcrowding and financial corruption. By 1815 matters had improved, but an investigation by another committee of MPs found much to complain about – dirt, overcrowding and a lack of fireplaces and glass in windows – but the abuses were much slighter.

Until the law changed in 1815, under the Gaol Fees Abolition Act, after a few years in prison debtors could be worse off than when they entered. Having no money had brought them to prison in the first place, but having to pay for their keep put them further into debt.

Ideas of prison reform were further promoted in the early nineteenth century by Elizabeth Fry and her brother Joseph John Gurney. In particular, Fry was appalled at the conditions in the women's section of Newgate Prison. The 1823 Gaols Act was

Preface

introduced and supported by the Home Secretary, Robert Peel. With other enactments, it stated that debtors should not be made to work without their consent and should never be made to work on the treadwheel.

Nevertheless, the general conditions in such prisons remained poor. The 1835 Prisons Act led eventually to their closure, ending a situation long considered to be a national scandal by contemporary commentators. The *Times* leader for 19 July 1844 offered the opinion:

> The law of debtor and creditor in this country is as yet, to use a geological metaphor, only in a transition state, and that a very unsatisfactory one. We are passing on from a state of barbarism into one of civilization, and have as yet only laid aside the blunt and butcherly weapons of the one, without having substituted the more polished, and it is to be hoped not less efficient, armoury of the other. Time was when any fraudulent concealment or embezzlement of his property and effects by a bankrupt was punishable with death as a felony; and, to use the words of Sir W. Blackstone, the great apologist for whatever was law in the reign of Queen Anne, 'unless it appeared that the inability of the bankrupt to pay his debts arose from some casual loss, he might, upon conviction by indictment of such gross misconduct and negligence, be set upon the pillory for two hours, and have one of his ears nailed to the same and cut off.' We have long since got rid of the pillory and the scaffold, and we are now, it is to be hoped, fast getting rid also of the hardly less inhuman practice of taking in execution indiscriminately the person of the debtor, without reference to the origin of his liabilities, whether in misfortune or in fraud. But we have as yet got nothing in the room of these things. We have now no indictments at all for fraud – no penal laws whatever against the polite pickpocket who steals duly under all the forms and regularities of law. We are renouncing the wholesale cruelty which with a uniform and general

Tracing Your Insolvent Ancestors

'Discovery of Jingle in the Fleet' by Phiz (Hablot Knight Browne), in Pickwick Papers *by Charles Dickens (1837).*

severity of punishment treats all, the unfortunate dupe as well as the designing knave, as alike guilty; and we have already renounced the mere savage brutalities which less refined times reserved for the particular distinction of fraud and knavery; but we are still as far as ever, or father from anything like a real and right discrimination between the guilty and the unfortunate, and we seem disposed now to frame our laws as if everybody were alike innocent.

In 1869 the Debtors' Act ended most imprisonment for debt, although a debtor who had the means to pay, but chose not to, could still be imprisoned for up to six weeks. Even today, there is a possibility that a debtor can be committed to prison as a consequence of litigation, but only for contempt of court by ignoring an actual court order. Protocol 4 of the current version of the European Convention on Human Rights now imposes a prohibition on imprisonment for debt.

A wealth of information exists on debtors and bankrupts. Records at The National Archives and local record offices will often throw light on a failed business venture, or those who suffered the ignominy of being branded a bankrupt or an insolvent debtor. We have come a long way from the days of debtors' prisons, with the introduction of the Companies Act and new bankruptcy laws, as well as Individual Voluntary Arrangements, Company Voluntary Arrangements, administration, receivership and so on. Many might argue that we still have some way to go. Debt and bankruptcy will probably always be with us, but the insolvent debtors of Dickens's time and before would certainly have appreciated the new rulebook.

Chapter 1

INSOLVENT DEBTORS – BACKGROUND

'Debt is the worst poverty' runs the old proverb. For some, debt was a way of life, while for others it was a state to be avoided at all costs. Nevertheless, tens of thousands whose finances were blighted by misfortunate or mismanagement appear in the records of the civil courts and debtors' prisons, and in local and national newspapers.

Unlike bankrupts, debtors were unable to more-or-less immediately wipe their slate clean and start over again. They remained burdened with their debts until these were either paid off or were waived by their creditors. In theory, being in debt was not a problem so long as the creditors did not complain. Understandably, most of them did, wielding the power to have their debtors imprisoned. Imprisonment for debt did not end until 1869.

In his 1691 book, *The Cry of the Oppressed*, Moses Pitt wrote:

> I here put into thy hand a small book, as full of tragedies as pages, which are not romances but truths, they are not acted in foreign nations among Turks and Infidels, Papists and Idolaters but in this our own country, by our own countrymen and relations to each other, not acted time out of mind by men many thousands or hundreds of years agone, but now at this very day by men now living in Prosperity, Wealth and Grandeur, they are such tragedies as no age or country can parallel. That men and women should be imprisoned all the

days of their lives by Bribers, Oppressors, Extortioners, Perjured persons etc. and these be Starving, Rotting with Soars and Carbuncles, Devoured with Vermin, Poisoned with Nasty Stinks, Knocked on the head and that for no crimes, but for their Misfortunes, Miscarriages and Losses by Trade and Merchandising which in no times or ages could be avoided nor care or industry prevent.

Unable to pay their debts, but still retaining responsibility for them, insolvent debtors were subject to common law proceedings and could be imprisoned until such time as they could discharge the debt. Consequently, debtors were routinely confined in either purpose-built debtors' prisons or in special sections of county gaols. There they would remain until the creditors had been satisfied or had cancelled the debt, possibly spending many years there, if not the rest of their lives.

The 'commercial traveller' in Charles Dickens's book *All the Year Round* (1867) only got out of prison because his father-in-law guaranteed his debts. Wives, left with no support, their husbands being incarcerated without any certainty of release, did on occasion resort to another, albeit bigamous, marriage.

Imprisonment was not intended as or seen as a punishment, but simply a way to secure the debtor, stopping him or her from moving away to avoid paying their creditors. It was also assumed that the threat of prison would encourage the debtor to find the funds from somewhere: from family or friends, or from assets which for some reason they would otherwise rather not have disclosed. Creditors believed that the potential disgrace of having a son or father incarcerated for an indefinite period would encourage their parents (or children) to open their wallets. In reality, creditors frequently gained no benefit from seeing their debtors sent to prison, where they were deprived of their livelihood and thus unable to earn sufficient money to pay off the debt.

So why did creditors take this course of action? In some cases, it was malice. In others, debtors had resources known to the creditor but simply refused to pay up. In 1844, there is an account of a prisoner who had been in Southampton Gaol for thirty years, simply because he refused to agree to the sale of some property which would have cleared his debts.

Nevertheless, the notion of being sent to prison for owing someone quite a small amount of money seems hard to believe today, but it was still happening well into Victorian times. The obvious major conceptual flaw with imprisoning debtors was that it then deprived them of the ability to earn money and so being able to pay off their creditors without resorting to friends or family. Dickens's 'commercial traveller' lost his position soon after being admitted to prison.

As the number of imprisoned debtors increased during the nineteenth century, changes to the law were introduced. Until 1827, it was possible for anyone owing £2 or more to be imprisoned, but the limit was then raised to £20. In 1844, an Act was passed to abolish imprisonment for those with small debts under £20. The following year, this apparent improvement in the lot of the small debtor was followed by legislation that effectively criminalized debtors for the first time. Courts were now able to imprison anyone with small debts of under £20 for forty days, if it could be proved that they were guilty of fraud by wilfully contracting a debt with the knowledge that they had no reasonable prospect of it being settled. In 1850, the value of a small debt was raised to £50.

From 1846, creditors could attempt to recover small debts through the County Court system. Court judgements routinely awarded the full claim, plus costs, to the creditor, with a series of payments by instalment being agreed. If the debtor subsequently defaulted on these payments, he or she was again liable to imprisonment.

Wealthy, and often famous, debtors had the great advantage that, if they were sufficiently quick-footed, they could flee to the Isle of Man or abroad. Lady Emma Hamilton took this course in 1814 when

Mr Dorrit is released from debtors' prison: 'The Marshalsea becomes an orphan' by Phiz (Hablot Knight Browne), in Little Dorrit *by Charles Dickens (1856)*

she moved to Calais in France. She was followed by Beau Brummel, who fled there in 1816. The fashionable haven was Boulogne. In 1857 there were 7,000 English there, about a quarter of the town's population.

A 1776 list of 'Fugitives King's Bench Prison' (Surrey History Centre: QS3/2/7) records several individuals identified as being abroad:

Job. Bull at Calais
Thomas Collis at Calais
Henry Daugard at Gothenburg in Sweden
James Harvey at Dunkirk
George Piggott at Guernsey
John William at Paris
Richard Jones at Dunkirk

Insolvent Debtors – Background

The English barrister, Sergeant Ballatine, described the debtors' life in Boulogne: 'many of them spent their days playing whist in a small club in the rue de l'Eau – occasionally one would have a big win and treat his friends to a large meal'. Even in Boulogne, many of the fugitives fell into further trouble and the local debtors' prison was nicknamed *l'Hotel Anglais*. In 1842, the English consul was reprimanded for spending ten times as much on helping distressed British subjects as the consul in Calais. When imprisonment for debt was abolished in 1869, many returned home and, according to Ballantine, 'much of the gaiety went out of the town'.

View of Boulogne port by Arnoult, mid-nineteenth century.

EXPOSING DEFAULTERS

Before the days of credit agencies and banks, credit cards and PayPal, householders and shopkeepers were regularly faced with the possibility of being defrauded. Credit was readily available from shopkeepers who were keen to attract additional business. Gentlemen's outfitters were renowned for giving credit to their upper- and middle-class clients. Many who took advantage of the credit offered found they were unable to pay off the debt or refused to do so. To take action against the debtor could be an expensive, tedious and lengthy business. There was no guarantee of a successful outcome, particularly if the debtor disappeared, possibly overseas, or filed for bankruptcy.

Just as today, some thought that the creditor was as guilty as the debtor. In a letter to *The Idler* in September 1758 the writer offered his view:

> The motive to credit is the hope of advantage. Commerce can never be at a stop, while one man wants what another can supply; and credit will never be denied, while it is likely to be repaid with profit. He that trusts one whom he designs to sue, is criminal by the act of trust; the cessation of such insidious traffic is to be desired, and no reason can be given why a change of the law should impair any other.

Several trade papers listed defaulters, such as the *Credit Drapers' Gazette*, often with their descriptions. From the late eighteenth century, a number of trade associations were formed which compiled and circulated to their members the details of known debtors, fraudsters and imposters. One of the earliest was the London-based 'The Guardians or, Society for the Protection of Trade against Swindlers and Sharpers', which was established on 25 March 1776. For an annual subscription of a guinea, members of the society received descriptive information about fraudsters and charlatans in the metropolis, particularly those who used false identities to obtain goods on credit.

Provincial Guardian Societies developed in the north of England from the 1820s, with the 'Manchester Guardian Society for the Protection of Trade', founded in 1826, enjoying particular success, issuing weekly reports on those seen as poor credit risks in the locality. In Birmingham, the 'Society for the Protection of Trade against fraudulent Bankrupts, Swindlers, etc.' was formed in 1804, to:

> prevent any flagrant attempts to impose on the honest and unwary, by fraudulent bankrupts and swindlers, and to detect cheats of every description; also, to prevent the friends and suspected accomplices of such persons from being appointed assignees or trustees, to the detriment of the creditors at large.

The Manchester Society established a debt-collection department to assist its members in 1850, a development which other Guardian Societies were quick to follow.

The National Archives has a set of printed handbills circulated to members of the London Society between 1825 and 1835, describing defaulters who had come to its attention and listing new members (C 114/34). Each handbill includes brief notes about individual debtors and swindlers. There is no standard format, and there might be just brief notes about the current activities of a known fraudster, or possibly a warning about a fictitious address being used by another.

For example, in April 1825 subscribers were informed about John Fitzwilliam Thistlewaite Hemsworth:

> That person has for some time been a Prisoner for Debt, in the Court Gaol of Warwick, from whence he sends his orders for Goods to various parts of the Kingdom. I am also directed to inform you that Piano Fortes of inferior make, and of little or no value, are frequently offered for sale, particularly at low Auctions, bearing names that have the same pronunciation as those of respectable makers, with the alteration, perhaps, or omission of a single letter, by which the Public are defrauded, and the character and reputation of the makers whose names are those pirated are lowered in general estimation; — thus

ROFE and Co., makers, Cheapside, London, instead of
ROLFE and Co., — now ROLFE and SONS who are the only makers of that name, known in London.

In November 1834, members were notified about another fraudster:

FREDERICK LANGLEY, 4 Old Quebec Street, Marylebone, and at other times leaving a card
HON. F. H. LANGLEY, ESQ. 11, Addison Road, Kensington. He is about 5 feet 6 inches in height, fair complexion, is of an insinuating address, but not much the appearance of a gentleman. He has to some given the names of FREDERICK LANGLEY, ESQ.

The careers of some well-known defaulters are described, most commonly after they had been discharged following a hearing under the Insolvent Debtors Act. The probable intent of these notices was to alert creditors of their release, and entries like this often give the trades in which they practised, with the addresses (often several) where they lived or from where they traded. In another example from November 1834 we find:

JOHN FREDERICK AUGUSTUS GRIESBACH, who represented himself as Owner of the Ship *Northumberland*, of which he stated a man named — WILDER was Captain, applied for his discharge lately under the Insolvent Debtors' Act, and was remanded.

Chapter 2

THE MACHINERY OF JUSTICE

The current judicial system in England and Wales is the result of 1,000 years of legal evolution. As a result, it is, and has been, both confusing and contradictory in places.

Prior to the nineteenth century, numerous courts were created to handle different branches of law. Some were relatively short-lived; others, performing similar tasks, were amalgamated over time; some survive, in one form or another, to the present day, continuing to exercise their original legal function.

Criminal law was concerned with offences against society at large – crimes – and these were prosecuted by the State, the intent being to punish and deter. Civil law was concerned with disputes between private parties: for example, consumer and supplier, employer and employee, creditor and debtor.

Today, we generally take it for granted that one of the functions of government is the administration of justice, which is generally expressed in terms of the sovereign: Queen's councillors, Queen's courts and HM prisons. But this was not always the case and the change, from pre-Conquest times to the present day, has been slow, protracted, complex and sometimes thorny.

Justice for the Anglo-Saxons, and in Norman times, was a combination of local and royal government. The King's court, the *curia regis*, was, initially at least, presided over by the king himself.

There were county-level courts and hundred courts, which had wide jurisdictions over both criminal and civil cases. There were manorial courts concerned with business within the manor itself.

And there were the ecclesiastical courts. The Quarter Sessions had the authority at county or borough level only. All were concerned with administrative matters in addition to the trying of cases.

There is no straightforward way of determining where any individual charged with being a debtor may have been tried. Britain's complicated legal system, with its hierarchy of courts, often resulted in there being several possibilities for the location of the trial. The same applied to any resulting release or conviction. The central civil law courts had jurisdiction over the whole of England and Wales. The Court of King's (Queen's) Bench, Court of Common Pleas, and the Plea Sides of the Chancery and Exchequer all attracted cases from any part of England and Wales. And there were several other smaller courts that developed over the centuries which may have seen cases of debt brought before them.

In London and the metropolis, the situation was possibly even more complicated. The civil law courts and sessions courts all had jurisdiction, but cases could also be heard at the Mayor's Court, Sheriff's Court or the City's own Court of Requests.

The usual legal process was for the debtor to be arrested by a bailiff or sheriffs' officer and then to be taken to what was called a 'sponging house'. In French, *éponger une dette* (sponge-up a debt) meant to repay one's debt. These houses were privately owned, often by the sheriffs' officers or their friends, and were often the officer's own home. The idea was to give the debtor a short time to attempt to settle his debts. While in the sponging house, debtors would be persuaded that they should pay up or face a court appearance and prison. They were notoriously uncomfortable, frequently filthy and badly run, as Mr Pickwick found:

> The coach having turned into a very narrow and dark street, stopped before a house with iron bars to all the windows; the door-posts of which were graced by the name and title of Namby, Officer to the Sheriffs of London; the inner gate having been opened by a gentleman who was endowed with a large

The Machinery of Justice

key for the purpose, Mr Pickwick was shown into the 'coffee-room'. This coffee-room was a front parlour, the principal features of which were fresh sand and stale tobacco smoke.

The sponging houses charged substantial fees: food and drink were additional charges and the debtor was not allowed to send out for supplies. This process was therefore usually of little benefit for the majority, as they would only have been there because they had no money. Often their hope was that friends or family would come forward to settle their total debt.

The 'commercial traveller' recounted in Charles Dickens's publication that:

> As a commercial traveller I can safely say that… the sum would have kept me a fortnight at any of the best hotels in London or the country.

'Morning and in Low Spirits – a Scene in a Lock up House' by Robert Cruickshank, in The English Spy, 1826.

In seven days at the sponging house in Bream's Buildings he spent £8 14s 6d, the main part being £1 a day for board and lodgings.

At the trial, debtors had to declare their assets. How these were to be applied was considered after consultation with the creditor or creditors.

In London, knowledge of the law was widespread. Many London plaintiffs appear to have attempted, often successfully, to procure perjured testimony in order to sustain a false prosecution. Such prosecutions frequently involved accusations of small debts, being promoted in order to encourage the victims to drop a prosecution of their own which was then in progress.

Another form of vexatious litigation was to swear a false accusation for debt, resulting in the victim facing imprisonment unless they could produce immediately a specified sum of money plus any associated fees. Offering a defence against such actions could be expensive and many victims found it more expedient to meet the demand of the plaintiff, although being entirely innocent of the charges. The Vexatious Arrests Act 1725, with other similar Acts, resulted in such prosecutions becoming more difficult as arrests for debts below 40 shillings became prohibited.

THE COURTS
The main three central common law courts that handled cases of debt, insolvency and bankruptcy were, until 1875:

- Court of Common Pleas
- The Exchequer of Pleas
- Court of the King's (Queen's) Bench, Plea Side

In addition to the three central common law courts, a number of other central courts also handled similar matters, including debt. These included the Courts of Equity:

- The Chancery Court

The Machinery of Justice

- Court of Requests
- Court of Star Chamber

and

- The Palace Court

The common law system also included:

- Assize Courts
- Palatinate of Lancaster Court of Common Pleas

At the local level, justice could be administered at numerous local courts. However, the main county or town courts were:

- Quarter Sessions
- Courts of Requests

The Court of Bankruptcy is considered in Chapter 11 and the Insolvent Debtors' Court in Chapter 9.

By the nineteenth century, competing jurisdictions, with their multiple forms of writs, had become unworkable and intolerable. In 1875, the whole machinery of justice was radically overhauled, with the creation of the Supreme Court of Judicature.

Common law courts
By the thirteenth century, three central courts – Common Pleas, Exchequer of Pleas, and the King's Bench – applied the common law. There was inevitably some overlapping of the jurisdictions of these bodies. But the principal difference was that disputes between subject and subject would be brought in the Court of Common Pleas, cases where the king was personally concerned went to the Court of King's Bench, and revenue cases went to the Exchequer of Pleas (or Court of Exchequer). These three, sitting in Westminster,

Westminster Hall, by Thomas Rowlandson in Ackermann's The Microcosm of London, *Vol.2, (1809).*

were collectively known as the 'common law' courts, to distinguish them from the ecclesiastical and other courts with special jurisdictions. Although the same law was applied in each court, they vied with each for other for business, particularly from the fifteenth century, claiming they offered better solutions for litigants.

The court machinery for civil cases was built around the writ system. A writ was a written order, made in the king's name and issued from the king's writing office, or chancery, at the request of the complainant (plaintiff). The defendant was ordered to appear in one of the royal courts or some inferior court that was charged with seeing justice done. The correct writ had to be selected to suit the form of the action.

To complicate matters, as early as 1285 it was provided that an action started in one of the Westminster courts would be set down to be tried there, 'unless first' (*nisi prius*) a justice should visit the county in question. The term Nisi Prius Court is still occasionally to be found used in connection with civil cases.

COURT OF COMMON PLEAS

The Court of Common Pleas had its origins in the *curia regis* (king's court) where, from 1178, a separate council heard pleas not involving the Crown. It remained a part of the *curia regis* until Magna Carta required that civil jurisdiction be assigned to a distinct body. In practice the court heard cases between subject and subject. These included all actions taken under *praecipe* (form of writ) to recover debts or property, which made up the clear majority of cases. Until 1558, under medieval common law, claims seeking the repayment of debt could only be pursued through a writ of debt in the Court of Common Pleas. Until the nineteenth century, the court was based in Westminster Hall, serving as one of the central English courts for 600 years, sitting regularly from 1249, although the court had maintained separate records from 1223.

In 1875 the court became a division of the High Court of Justice, and in 1881 its jurisdiction passed to Queen's Bench Division.

Court of King's Bench, by Thomas Rowlandson in Ackermann's The Macrocosm of London, *Vol.2, (1809).*

Court of King's (or Queen's) Bench

The Court of King's Bench (or Queen's Bench during the reign of a female monarch) was a court of common law created in the late twelfth and early thirteenth century from the *curia regis*. It initially followed the monarch on his travels until the early fifteenth century, but had mostly settled at Westminster Hall from 1318 where it sat until the nineteenth century. The first records of an independent King's Bench date from 1234.

The court functioned as the highest court of common law, handling matters that directly concerned the king or related to maintaining the 'king's peace', eventually including all types of personal action. Although the court had some criminal jurisdiction, its main jurisdiction was over 'pleas of the crown': cases which involved the king in some way. This was with the exception of revenue matters, which were handled by the Exchequer of Pleas.

Claims seeking the repayment of debt were restricted to the Court of Common Pleas until 1558. From then, another method of recovering debts became available, enforced by the Court of King's Bench. This was through the action of *assumpsit*, which was technically for deceit. The legal fiction used was that by failing to pay, after promising to do so, a defendant had committed deceit, and was liable to the plaintiff.

By the time of the accession of Queen Anne in 1702, the court was organized into two parts, the 'crown side', where criminal cases were considered, and the 'plea side' for the consideration of personal actions, including debt. Thenceforth the records of the court were divided accordingly.

Under the Supreme Court of Judicature Acts, the Queen's Bench ceased to exist, holding its last session on 6 July 1875.

EXCHEQUER OF PLEAS OR COURT OF EXCHEQUER

The Exchequer was established around 1118 as a royal court based in London, whose main concern was calling in debts owed to the monarch. The court dealt with matters of equity, a set of legal principles based on natural law and common law in England and Wales. The Court split from the *curia regis* during the 1190s to sit as an independent, central court.

The Exchequer's position as a court originally came from processing disputes between the king and his debtors as to how much money was owed. By the thirteenth century this had evolved into formal court proceedings. Initially, this was as a court where only the king could bring cases, but this developed to allow debtors to collect on their own debts in the Exchequer, so that they could better pay the king.

The Insolvent Debtors Act 1820, establishing the Court of Bankruptcy, removed cases of insolvency from the Exchequer. In 1875 it became a separate division of the High Court of Justice, and in 1881 that division was amalgamated with the Queen's Bench Division.

Equity courts
Chancery Court
Many would-be litigants were wary of the common law courts, believing they would not or could not give them reasonable and unbiased 'equitable' justice. They would therefore petition the king or his council. By the late-fifteenth century, petitions were being directed to the chancellor. By this point the Court of Chancery had evolved, the guiding principle of which was 'conscience rather than the implementation of existing law'. Consequently, the Chancery Court held a common law jurisdiction through its plea side, covering relations between Crown and subject – this included an increasing role in debt jurisdiction on actions for recognisances for debt entered in Chancery.

Court of Requests
The Court of Requests was established in 1483 to provide easy access for poor men and women to royal justice and equity. It was known as the Court of Poor Men's Causes until 1529. Because of the limited expense of bringing suit before it, the court was a popular choice, providing a cheap and simple procedure attracting many suitors, not all of them poor, but a significant number of them women.

The Court of Requests was mainly concerned with civil matters – title to land, covenants, annuities and debt – though it sometimes handled criminal cases such as forgery and riot.

It was resented by the lawyers of the common law courts who were concerned about the loss of business, and therefore income, that resulted from its popularity. From 1590 a series of prohibitions from the Court of Common Pleas reduced business in the Court of

Requests. Although the court was never formally abolished, it effectively did not survive after the Restoration of the monarchy in 1660, with the records of the court ending in 1642.

COURT OF STAR CHAMBER

From the late fifteenth century, a number of smaller courts with specific authorities were established, including the Court of Star Chamber. These were all abolished in 1641.

On the whole, the court presided over criminal cases, but did also exercise some civil jurisdiction, including cases involving debt. In the 1530s the Star Chamber dealt with about 150 cases a year, and its business expanded significantly over the following decades, so that by 1600 it was presiding over nearly 700 cases a year.

Palace Court

In 1630, Charles I created a new court called the Palace Court, or *Curia Palatii*, having jurisdiction to hear all kinds of personal actions between parties within twelve miles of Whitehall Palace, which did not fall within the jurisdiction of the City of London or other liberties. The court sat in Southwark, in Surrey, until early in the nineteenth century when it moved to Scotland Yard, Westminster.

The Palace Court in practice came to deal mainly with suits for the recovery of small debts, ranging between its lower limit, 40 shillings, and £5–£10 from 1725 and £20 from 1827. Use of the court had rapidly declined some time before its abolition at the end of 1849, under the County Courts Act of that year.

Assize courts

Importantly, the common law system also included the Assize courts. From early Norman times, representatives of the king had travelled to the counties for a variety of purposes. Eventually, their judicial activities became the main purpose of their visits and they became itinerant justices, visiting each county three or four times a year.

Virtually all criminal trials took place in the county where the crime was committed, as did civil cases where the sum was small (under 40 shillings). All cases considered to be of importance were referred to one of the common law courts in Westminster. The Assize courts rarely, if ever, handled cases of debt unless there was some criminal aspect to the case.

Palatinate of Lancaster Court of Common Pleas

The Court of Common Pleas for the county of Lancaster was a further common law court that had jurisdiction where the defendant was resident in Lancashire, although the action may have arisen elsewhere. Cases of debt brought to the court were only where the defendant owed less than £20. The court sat in Lancaster before one of the two judges assigned to the Northern Circuit. The court was absorbed into the Supreme Court of Judicature under the 1873 and 1875 Acts.

Supreme Court of Judicature

The Supreme Court of Judicature Acts 1873 and 1875, which came into effect on 1 November 1875, brought about the replacement of the three common law courts, as well as the assumption of equity jurisdiction. The three central common law courts became three of the five divisions of the Supreme Court: Queen's Bench Division, Common Pleas Division, Exchequer Division, together with the Chancery Division, and the Admiralty, Probate, and Divorce and Matrimonial Causes Division.

From 1881, the Exchequer and Common Pleas divisions were amalgamated with the Queen's Bench Division. The London Court of Bankruptcy became the High Court of Justice in Bankruptcy in 1883.

This current guide to insolvent debtors, with some exceptions, does not generally cover the records for this later period, from 1875 up to the present day.

Chapter 3

RELIEF AND RELEASE

Queen Anne's Act to Relieve Insolvent Debtors in 1711 had stated that debtors could discharge a portion of their liabilities which would then enable them to be released from imprisonment. One clause required the publication of insolvency notices in the *Gazette*. Within a few weeks, these notices began to appear, and in the issue for Monday 3 June 1712 we find:

> Charles Thomas, Prisoner in the Compter in the County of Surry, having petitioned one of her Majesty's Justices of the Peace in the said County, and his Warrant signed thereupon, directed to the Goaler of the said Prison, to bring the said Thomas to the General Quarter Sessions held for the said County at Guildford, on the 15th of July next to be discharged, pursuant to an Act lately passed, for Relief of Insolvent Debtors; and he conforming himself in all things as the Act directs, his respective Creditors are to take Notice thereof.

The abuses in the prisons and the absurdity of locking up people who could not pay their bills led to a campaign for reform which lasted for many years. The reformers were opposed by tradesmen who saw debtors' prison as a valuable threat to people who would not settle what they were owed. In the eighteenth century a number of Acts were passed which allowed insolvent debtors to be released if they applied to a court and transferred all their assets to their creditors. However, if a debtor was released under this legislation, any future property could also be seized by his creditors.

The preamble to the Discharge of Insolvent Debtors Act 1794 stated:

Whereas, notwithstanding the great prejudice and detriment which acts of insolvency produce to trade and credit, it may be convenient, in the present condition of the gaols in this kingdom, that some of the prisoners who are now confined therein should be set at liberty.

The Act therefore required that those in debt to a sum not exceeding £1,000 should be released after taking an oath. Gaolers were also ordered to make out lists of all debtors in prison on 12 February 1794.

John Howard commented that while the 1747 Act for the Relief of Insolvent Debtors had enabled some debtors to obtain, by a legal process, one groat (4 pence) per day for their relief in gaol, only twelve debtors in the whole of England and Wales managed to achieve this because generally the means of procuring it were outside their reach.

On one of his journeys, Howard found 600 prisoners whose debts were under £20, some of whom did not owe more than £3 or £4. The expense in trying to obtain this financial help was often equal to the small debts for which they had been confined in the first place. At Carlisle, only one debtor of the forty-nine that he saw had obtained his groats and the gaoler had told him that during the fourteen years that he had been in office, only four or five prisoners had received it. Howard summed up the conditions for debtors as, 'The truth is some debtors are the most pitiable objects in our gaols'.

Under An Act for the Discharge out of Prison such Insolvent Debtors, as shall serve or Procure a person to serve in Her Majesty's Fleet or Army, 1704, debtors could be discharged 'according to the tenour of the said Act' so long as the creditors and gaolers could not produce good reason to the contrary. Local record offices may have lists of those who took advantage of the offer.

CHARITY

The plight of the very many genuinely poor imprisoned debtors was recognized by several charities. In addition to applying for money from these charities, prisoners resorted to begging. The Fleet Prison in London had an alms box at the gate and paupers would go about the prison with a begging box and were, as a consequence, described as being 'on the box'.

By the beginning of the nineteenth century, the number of prisoners who were reduced to the begging grate had declined significantly. The probable reason for this was the activities of the Society for the Discharge and Relief of Persons Imprisoned for Small Debts – more usually known as Thatched House, from its regular meeting place, the Thatched House Tavern, or the Craven Street Society. The Society was founded in 1772 on the initiative of the prison reformer James Neild (1744–1814), a London jeweller. He believed most fell into debt because of bad luck rather than bad character and did not think imprisonment a valid approach. In February 1772, he heard an inspirational sermon by the Reverend Weeden Butler and subsequently set up a fundraising committee. The resulting £81 settled the debts and secured the release of thirty-four prisoners.

The society was at first concerned with London prisons only and the greatest number of debtors came from these, but by the 1780s prisoners from gaols in other parts of the country were also being assisted. At their meetings, the society considered petitions for financial aid from debtors owing less than £10. Good moral character and sobriety were required of claimants. Part of the society's ethos was that creditors had a spiritual and moral duty to work compassionately with debtors rather than against them, and so it would only pay part of the amount owed to them. From 1772 to 1831 the society enabled 51,250 people, usually men with families, to discharge their debts and rejoin society, and spent £164,000 in doing so, at an average cost of just under £3.

At The National Archives there some records of the Thatched House Society:

Petitions for discharge and declarations of destitution. Replies to prisoner's petitions	No dates	PRIS 10/238
Replies to prisoners' petitions	1844–1845	PRIS 10 238/5

Other records of the Thatched House Society are held at London Metropolitan Archives:

Minutes	1772–1941	A/RSD/01/001-022
General expenditure books	1830–1879	A/RSD/07/001-007
Rules and orders	1827–1873	A/RSD/16/001-002
Acts of Parliament	1740–1824	A/RDS/04A/001, A/RSD/23/001-007
Histories of the Society	1774–1993	A/RSD/15/001-002, A/RSD/25/001-004

Early volumes of the minute books and general expenditure books include the names of discharged debtors.

The society did occasionally refuse to help prisoners where there was evidence that they had behaved fraudulently or had not helped themselves to obtain release. The problem was that if a person had been imprisoned for debt, his creditor could not seize his property. Some people preferred to go to a debtors' prison in order to protect their property against seizure. In 1782 the Society refused assistance to Bernard Shield and James Smelley in the Marshalsea because they had disputed past debts and had remained in prison.

Neild secured the support of social reformers, such as William Wilberforce, and Earl Romney became the president of the society. George III gave £2,000 to the society as part of the celebrations to mark his Golden Jubilee in 1810. The society also acted as a pressure

Relief and Release

group, arguing for better conditions for prisoners. By the nineteenth century it was still writing letters to governors of local prisons. In 1828, the society successfully drove a corrupt governor of Whitecross Street out of office. James Neild went on to publish *The State of the Prisons in England, Scotland and Wales* (1812).

COURT FOR THE RELIEF OF INSOLVENT DEBTORS

In 1813, the Court for the Relief of Insolvent Debtors was set up. This allowed for the release of prisoners on condition they surrendered all their property for the benefit of their creditors. The court was not a great success, as from the debtors' point of view it was expensive and left them with an uncertain future, since further property they might acquire could be made available to creditors. Its processes were complex and expensive, but it did provide a way out of prison for people who might otherwise have had no escape.

Peter Cunningham, in his *Hand-Book of London* (1850) commented:

> The Insolvent Debtors Court, or Court for the Relief and Discharge of Insolvent Debtors, is in Portugal Street, Lincoln's-inn-Fields. The principle upon which it is established is this: the person is for ever released, but the property never, as long as any claims remain unsatisfied.

At Lancaster Prison it was reported that of the 174 people imprisoned for debt that year, only sixteen obtained their freedom by paying off what was owed.

Debtors or traders who owed very little could petition for protection orders. These were registered by the Court of Bankruptcy from 1842 to 1847, and the Court for the Relief of Insolvent Debtors from 1847 to 1861. TNA holds some of these records, and those for insolvent debtors imprisoned outside London can be found at local archives.

In Charles Dickens's *David Copperfield*, Mr Micawber is sent to the King's Bench Prison in London. Under the Act for the Relief of

Insolvent Debtors, Micawber applies for his release and is discharged.

Under the Bankruptcy Act 1847, jurisdiction over both traders and non-traders owing less than £300 passed to the Court for the Relief of Insolvent Debtors (established by the Insolvent Debtors (England) Act 1813) in both London and the County Courts elsewhere.

CIRCUITS
OF THE
Commissioners for the Relief of Insolvent Debtors.

1847. SUMMER CIRCUITS.	Southern Circuit. H. R. REYNOLDS, Esq. Chief Commissioner.	Northern Circuit. J. G. HARRIS, Esq. Commissioner.	Midland Circuit. W. J. LAW, Esq. Commissioner.	Home Circuit. C. PHILLIPS, Esq. Commissioner.
Friday, June 18		Sheffield		
Monday, 21		Wakefield		
Tuesday, 22	Reading			
Thursday, 24	Oxford		Chelmsford	
Friday, 25		Kingston-upon-Hull	Colchester	
Saturday, 26	Worcester			
Monday, 28		York	Ipswich	
Tuesday, 29	Presteigne		Norwich	
Wednesday, 30	Hereford			
Thursday, July 1		Richmond	Yarmouth	
Friday, 2	Brecon	Durham		
Saturday, 3			Bury St. Edmunds	
Monday, 5	Carmarthen	Newcastle upon Tyne	Lynn	
Tuesday, 6			Peterborough	
Wednesday, 7	Cardigan	Carlisle	Huntingdon	
Thursday, 8	Haverfordwest		Cambridge	Dover
Friday, 9		Appleby		
Saturday, 10		Kendal	Northampton	Canterbury
Monday, 12	Swansea	Lancaster	Oakham	
Tuesday, 13	Cardiff		Lincoln	Maidstone
Thursday, 15	Monmouth		Nottingham	
Saturday, 17	Gloucester		Derby	
Monday, 19		Liverpool	Leicester	
Tuesday, 20	Bristol			
Wednesday, 21			Stafford	
Thursday, 22	Bath	Welsh Pool		
Friday, 23	Taunton		Shrewsbury	
Saturday, 24		Dolgelly	Lichfield	
Monday, 26			Oldbury	
Same day,			Birmingham	
Tuesday, 27	Bodmin	Carnarvon	Warwick	
Wednesday, 28	Plymouth	Beaumaris	Coventry	
Friday, 30	Exeter	Ruthin	Bedford	Lewes
Saturday, 31			Aylesbury	
Monday, August 2	Dorchester	Mold		
Tuesday, 3		Chester		
Wednesday, 4	Salisbury			
Thursday, 5	Southampton			
Friday, 6	Winchester			Hertford

Hodson Printer to the Court Clifford's Inn passage Fleet Street London.

Circuits of the Commissioners for the Relief of Insolvent Debtors, Summer Circuits, 1847.

Relief and Release

Outside London, these matters were handled by county courts. Sometimes, Insolvent Debtors' Courts sat with commissioners deciding the cases. Quarter Sessions records at local record offices usually hold this information. Debtors had to declare their assets and their application was considered after consultation with the creditors.

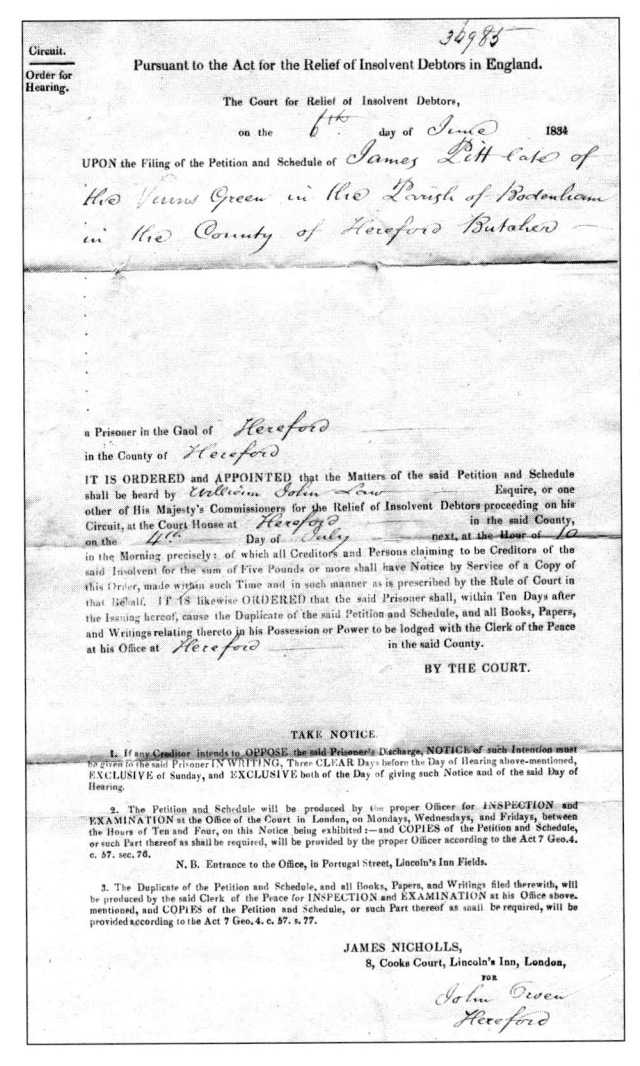

Order for hearing the petition of James Pitt of Bodenham, Herefordshire, butcher, a prisoner in Hereford Gaol; dated 6 June 1835; pursuant to the 'Act for the Relief of Insolvent Debtors in England'.

The Bankruptcy Act 1861 ended the distinction between bankrupts and insolvent debtors. The Court for the Relief of Insolvent Debtors was abolished, and its jurisdiction was transferred to the Bankruptcy Court. It authorized registrars of the Court of Bankruptcy to visit prisons and adjudge bankrupt those imprisoned for debt who satisfied them as to the genuineness of their insolvency. This resulted in a dramatic fall in the number of debtors in prison. By 1877, only 3.1 per cent of all committals to prison were for debt.

The Debtors' Act, as a Bill, did not include any clause for retaining the power of imprisonment. A clause was only inserted during the parliamentary debate, probably as a result of representations made by a deputation of county court judges. At the time, these judges had little to do except sit at debt-collecting cases and were therefore fearful that if committal was completely abolished, their work, and income, would decline.

In the same year, the Bankruptcy Act abolished the provincial District Bankruptcy Courts, their jurisdiction passing to the county courts; the jurisdiction of the Court of Bankruptcy was now confined to causes arising in London and was afterwards known as the London Court of Bankruptcy. The Act established the first statutory regime for preferential debts in bankruptcy, which included local and central taxes as well as wages and salaries of clerks, servants, labourers and workers. In certain cases of bankruptcy where fraud was proved, the bankrupt could be imprisoned for two years.

The London Court of Bankruptcy was incorporated into the Supreme Court of Judicature in 1883 and renamed the High Court of Justice in Bankruptcy. In the same year, provision was made for the official receiver of the Board of Trade to assume control of all a debtor's property in the interests of creditors.

The surviving records of the Court for Relief of Insolvent Debtors and the Court of Bankruptcy are also at TNA. These are fully detailed in Chapter 4 and Chapter 10 with the other records relating to debtors held there. Records relating to London prisoners may be held at London Metropolitan Archives (see Chapter 8) or in local

Relief and Release

archives and record offices around the country (see Chapter 9).

As an illustration of what can be found, Warwickshire Record Office holds information on two contrasting debtors. Thomas Mann, of Norton Lindsey in Warwickshire, had been a High Constable of the county until 1841 when, at the Easter Quarter Sessions, he was dismissed for not paying the county's rates. In Coventry, in December 1842, the Court for the Relief of Insolvent Debtors heard that Mann owed £555 6s and had paid only £100 at the Clerk of the Peace's Office, Stratford-on-Avon.

Early in 1842, James Beck, the County Treasurer, made an affidavit that Mann had not paid an outstanding £255 16s. A warrant was issued to send him to prison. By July 1842 he had applied to be discharged under the Act for the Relief of Insolvent Debtors, but a brief exists to show that the county opposed it.

A responsible county officer, Mann was clearly not a run-of-the-mill debtor. The Insolvent Debtors Court felt that Mann had used the rates he received for his own purpose and therefore opposed his release.

Chapter 4

INSOLVENT DEBTORS – COURT AND COURT RECORDS

The descriptions on Discovery (discovery.nationalarchives.gov.uk) of the records held by The National Archives include many references to records for each of the common law courts, as well as several other courts of law. However, many descriptions, where they are included, can be difficult to comprehend, particularly for the non-expert in legal matters or terminology. It is therefore advisable, at least in the early stages of research, to concentrate on just a few of the more important Series, especially if one or more of these can act as indexes to other records for the same court and period being researched.

Importantly, the descriptions of the records on Discovery can be very detailed and extremely informative. These should always be read before considering ordering a specific document from a particular Series, as they can often provide comprehensive information on the records and can indicate other records of relevance that could be consulted.

> **DISCOVERY**
> Discovery is The National Archives' catalogue. It provides a way to explore the archival collections held at The National Archives itself, and also at over 2,500 other archives across the UK.
>
> Discovery has been designed to host, search and display the many different databases and datasets held at both The National Archives and other archives. It therefore provides a single portal

for information that might otherwise only be found by investigating numerous other websites.

Discovery is the catalogue of over 22 million historical government and public records, of which nine million are digitized and available to download. TNA's own collections include paper and parchment, electronic records and websites, photographs, posters, maps, drawings and paintings, dating from the Domesday Book to modern government papers and digital files.

However, the catalogues of the local archives integrated into Discovery are taken from some outdated datasets and will possibly have been superseded by the current catalogues held by the individual archives themselves. Therefore, whereas the material found on Discovery may act as a good indicator of what is to be found beyond TNA, the catalogues of the provincial archives need to be consulted for more accurate and up-to-date descriptions of what is held at a local level.

In general, the descriptions on Discovery of each of the record Series held at TNA are the most detailed and up-to-date descriptions available. Clarification of the historical and legal background to the records, as well as their physical description and instances of variation from the norm, are essential for a full understanding of the records and an essential requirement in using them to a much greater depth than can be covered here.

The most important Series of records include the Plea Rolls, which record the formal business of the courts. The rolls are made up of many individual 'rotuli' (singular 'rotulus') on which are outlined the nature of the action, an account of the process and the final judgement, if one was made. The rolls can also include the texts of any deeds enrolled in the court. *Posteas* Files record the trial proceeding and the verdict in a civil process. Many Plea Rolls, and other Series, are not kept on site at Kew and require three working days' notice to be delivered from the DeepStore repository in Winsford, Cheshire.

COMMON LAW COURTS
Court of Common Pleas

Plea Rolls	1194–1272	KB 26
Plea Rolls	1273–1874	CP 40
Warrants of Attorneys to Confess Judgements	1802–1849, 1866–1874	CP 48
Protonotaries Docket Rolls	1509–1770, 1791–1859	CP 60
Entry Books of Judgements; Indexes to Entry Books of Judgements	1859–1874	CP 64
Docket Books	1660–1839	IND 1/6373-6605
Indexes to Debtors and Accountants to the Crown	1839-1900	CP 16

The earliest Plea Rolls, 1194 to 1272, are now in Series KB 26. The Plea Rolls from 1273–1874, CP 40 are made up of many numbered rotuli. The rolls are arranged by year and law term. There are no indexes, but reference to the individual rotulus numbers can be found in other Series of the court's records and the entries on Discovery are cross-referenced to those for both IND 1 and CP 60. The Docket Books, 1660–1839, IND 1/6373-6605 give the rotulus numbers of cases reaching judgement. The entries on Discovery for IND 1 are cross-referenced to those for CP 40.

The largest source is the Series of Protonotaries Docket Books, 1509–1770 & 1791–1859, CP 60. The entries on Discovery for CP 60 are also cross-referenced to those for CP 40.

CP 64 are Entry Books of Judgements, 1859–1874, with indexes in the same Series.

CP 16 comprises an Index to Debtors and Accountants to the Crown. The records in this Series were established in 1839. They include details of persons whose estates would be affected by any

Insolvent Debtors – Court and Court Records

arrangement which would leave them with a debt to the Crown. The volumes give details of name, address, title/profession, type of transaction, date, and the amount of debt, damages or costs. The requirement to keep an index was abolished in 1900.

Warrants of Attorney to Confess Judgement, 1802–1849 & 1866–1874, CP 48 are warrants, mostly in cases of debt, made by defendants to attorneys, allowing judgement to be conceded against them. Filed with them can be details of the financial terms required by the defendant.

Example 1: Hilary term, 8 George II (1735)

In 1735, Henry Tasker brought an action against Mary Calley of Swansombe in Kent, for the repayment of a debt of £70. The entry in the Docket Book (IND 1/6492) records the amount of the debt, £70 and damages, £60, and the Plea Roll rotulus number, 1784:

| Calley | George Hunt Clerk to answer Mary late of Swanscombe in ye County af^d Widow otherwise called

~~~~~To answer Henry Tasker | 70 | 60 | 1784 | Kent |

The Docket Roll entry (CP 60/1148) is less informative than that in the Docket Book:

| Kent | Not informed in Deb^t

Tasker for Tasker

Matthews for Calley | 1784 |

The Plea Roll (CP 40/3460 rot.1784) gives full details of the case brought by Henry Tasker against Mary Calley:

Kent to witt
Mary Calley late of Swanscombe in the County aforesd Widow otherwise called Mary Calley of Greenhithe in the parish of

Plea Roll, Mary Calley v Henry Tasker.

Swanscombe in the County of Kent was summoned to Answer Henry Tasker in a Plea that she render to him Seventy pounds which she Owes him and unjustly detains from him And wherefore the sd Henry by John Tasker his Attorney Complains That Whereas the said Mary the Twenty fifth day of November in the Eighth Year of the Reign of the now King at Dartford in the County aforesaid by her certain Bond or Writing Obligatorie bearing date the same day and year

Insolvent Debtors – Court and Court Records

Certified herself held and firmly bound unto the said Henry Tasker in the sd Seventy pounds to be paid to the same Henry when thereunto afterwards requested yet the sd Mary (although thereunto often times requested) hath not rendered the sd Seventy pounds to the sd Henry but hath hitherto denied and yet denyeth to render that Sum to him Whereupon the sd Henry saith he is prejudiced and hath Damage to the value of Twenty pounds and thereupon he brings Suit And the said Henry brings here into Court the writing aforesd which prove the sd Debt in forme aforesd The Date of which is the day and year aforesaid.

And the said Mary by John Mathews her Attorney cometh and Defendeth the force and Injury when &c. And the said Attorney saith that he is not informed by the sd Mary of any Answer of the sd Mary to be given to the sd Henry in the Complaint afd and saith nothing more whereby the said Henry remaineth against the sd Mary therefore undefended Therefore it is Adjudged that the sd Henry should recover against the sd Mary his Debt afd and his Damages by reason of the Detaining of that Debt adjudged By this Court to the sd Henry with his Assent to Sixty Shillings And the sd Mary in Mercy and so forth.

Signed the 21st March 1734

EXAMPLE 2: MICHAELMAS TERM, 56 GEORGE III (1815)

In 1815, Rebecca Farmer made a claim against George Hunt Holley, sometime Rector of Hactor with Whitwell, Norfolk, for a debt of £990 which she asserted was owed her by him.

The entry in the Docket Book (IND 1/6581) records the amount of the debt, £900 and damages, £80, and the Plea Roll number, 537:

| Holley | George Hunt Clerk to answer Rebecca Farmer | 900 | 80 | 537 | Norfolk |

The Docket Roll entry (CP 60/1148) is less informative than that in the Docket book:

Norfolk	Says nothing in Deb^t	537
	Farmer Plt	
	Holley Deff	

The Plea Roll (CP 40/3895 rot.537) gives full details of the case brought by Rebecca Farmer against George Hunt Holley:

In the Common Pleas
Michaelmas Term in the fifty-six year of the reign of King George the Third Norfolk to wit George Hunt Holley Clerk was summoned to answer Rebecca Farmer in a plea that he render to the said Rebecca nine hundred Pounds of lawful money of Great Britain which he owes to and unjustly detains from her and thereupon the said Rebecca by Thomas Holloway her attorney complains That whereas the said George Hunt on the first day of December in the year of our Lord one thousand eight hundred and fifteen to wit at Norwich in the County of Norfolk aforesaid borrowed of the said Rebecca the said sum of nine hundred Pounds above demanded to be paid to her the said Rebecca when he the said George Hunt should be thereunto afterwards requested Yet the said George Hunt although often requested &c. hath not yet paid the said sum of nine hundred pounds above demanded or any part thereof to the said Rebecca but he to pay the same or any part thereof hath hitherto wholly refused and still refuses wherefore the said Rebecca says she is injured and hath sustained damage to the value of nine hundred Pounds and therefore she brings her suit &c

And the said George Hunt by Faithful Croft his attorney comes And defends the wrong and injury when &c and says nothing in bar or preclusion of the said action of the said

Insolvent Debtors – Court and Court Records

Rebecca by which the said Rebecca remains therein undefended against the said George Hunt Therefore it is considered that the said Rebecca recover against the said George Hunt her said debt and also eighty shillings for her damages which she hath sustained as well by occasion of the detaining the said Debt as for her Costs and Charges by her about her suit in this behalf expended by the Court here adjudged to the said Rebecca by her assent and the said George Hunt in mercy &c

Judgment signed 5 December 1815

Lastly, the Warrant of Attorneys to Confess Judgements for George Hunt Holley survives (CP 38/74):

To Thomas Holloway and Faithful Croft
~~~~~~~ Attorneys to his Majesty's Court of Common Pleas at Westminster jointly and severally or to any other Attorney of the same Court

These are to desire and authorize you the Attorneys above named or any one of you or any other Attorney of the Court of Common Pleas ~~~~~~~ aforesaid To appear for me George Hunt Holley late of Vale Place Hammersmith Clerk as of Michaelmas Term last past Hilary Term next or any subsequent Term

And then and there issue a Declaration for me in an Action of debt upon Demand for nine hundred pounds Money borrowed ~~~~~~~ at the Suit of Rebecca Farmer of Vale Place Hammersmith Widow her Exors or Admors
[…]
In Witness whereof I ~~~~~~~ have hereunto set my hand and Seal the first ~~~~~~~ Day of December ~~~~~~~ in the fifty sixth Year of the Reign of our Sovereign Lord George the third by the Grace of God
[…]

This Warrant of Attorney is given to secure the payment of four hundred and ninety pounds due and owing by the said George Hunt Holley to the said Rebecca Farmer with lawful Interest from this day and it is agreed that Judgement may be entered up forthwith but that no Execution shall be issued unless default be made in payment of the said £490 + Interest on the 26th day of December which will be in the year of our Lord one thousand Eight hundred and Sixteen

Example 3: Easter term, 22 Victoria (1859)

A final example from the Court Common Pleas, from 1859, involved a debt owed to Edward Brettle, George Henry Brettle and Thomas Wilson Elstob by Henry Longman.

The Docket Roll entry (CP 60/1183) names the plaintiff and defendants, and supplies the Plea Roll number, 305:

England	Brettle & ors plts	
12 July	Longman deft	305
1859	Matthews for Calley	

The Plea Roll (CP 40/4069 rot.305) gives full details of the case brought by Edward Brettle, George Henry Brettle and Thomas Wilson Elstob against Henry Longman:

In the Common Pleas
On the tenth day of May in the year of our Lord One thousand eight hundred and fifty nine.
England (to wit) Edward Brettle George Henry Brettle and Thomas Wilson Elstob by George Henley Barber their Attorney sued out a writ of Summons against Henry Longman indorsed as follows. The Plaintiffs claim £70.0.2 principal and interest due to them as the Drawers of a Bill of Exchange of which the following is a copy

Insolvent Debtors – Court and Court Records

[...]
The Plaintiffs also claim interest on the above sum of £69.11.6 at £5 per cent per annum from date of Writ until payment or Judgement And £2.15/- for costs. And if the amount thereof be paid to the Plaintiffs or to their Attorneys within four days from the service hereof further proceedings will be stayed And the said Henry Longman has not appeared Therefore, it is considered that the said Edward Brettle George Henry Brettle and Thomas Wilson Estob recover against the said Henry Longman Seventy pounds Three shillings and eleven pence together with Four pounds for costs of suit
  Signed 10th May 1859

The Entry Book of Judgements, CP 64/85 records Henry Longman as the defendant, Brettle and others as plaintiffs, with total damages of £73.3.11:

| 10th May Longman | Henry | Brettle & ors | 74 | 3 | 11 | E[ngland] |

Court of King's (Queen's) Bench

Plea Rolls (plea side and Crown side)	1194–1272 (5 Richard I – 56 Henry III)	KB 26
Plea Rolls (plea side and Crown side)	1273–1702 (Edward I – William III)	KB 27
Plea Rolls (plea side only)	1702–1876 (1 Anne – 39 Victoria)	KB 122
Docket Books	1656–1839	IND 1
Entry Books of Judgements	1699–1875	KB 168

Indexes to Entry Books of Judgements	1736–1875	KB 168
Warrants of Attorney to Confess Judgement	1802–1825	KB 128

Early Plea Rolls, 1194–1272, are in KB 26. For the period 1656–1839, the Docket Books, IND 1 can be used to locate the relevant entry in the Plea Rolls, KB 27, KB 122. These provide alphabetical lists of the defendants' names together with the relevant rotulus number in the Plea Rolls. From 1760, it became less common for all rotuli to be filed in the Plea Rolls and by 1841 it is estimated that only about 10 per cent were being filed. The entries on Discovery for the Plea Rolls and Docket Books cross-reference each other.

The Entry Books of Judgements, 1699–1875, together with their associated indexes, 1736–1875, both KB 168, not only act as a means of reference to the Plea Rolls, but are also a partial substitute for the missing enrolments from 1760. These are arranged chronologically giving the date, county, plaintiffs' and defendants' names, attorneys' names, and brief details of the sum in dispute. The Indexes are to the names of the defendants.

The catalogue entries on TNA's Discovery can be particularly helpful as the Plea Rolls, Docket Books and Entry Books of Judgements are all cross-referenced, within the relevant time periods, making it reasonably straightforward to identify the correct pieces to order up.

The Warrants of Attorney to Confess Judgement, KB 28 begins in 1802, when the court stipulated that the warrant should be filed with the clerk of the dockets and judgments.

EXAMPLE 1: TRINITY TERM, 6 GEORGE I (1720)
William Cullock made a claim against Edward Hancock. However, as the records date to 1720, the entries are in Latin.

The entry in Discovery for the 1720 Docket Book includes reference to the related Plea Roll (KB 122):

Docket Book to KB 122/94 – KB 122/95, Court of King's Bench Plea (Judgment) Roll, 6 Geo I, Easter term to 6 Geo I, Trinity term

Easter to Trinity 6 Geo 1 covers roughly the period March to July 1620. The entry in the Docket Book includes the rotulus number, 499 in the Plea Roll (KB 122/95).

The cause is also included in the *Entry Book of Judgements Trinity Term 1620* (KB 168/4).

The entry in the Plea Roll for Trinity Term, 1720 (KB 122/95 rot.499) details the action between Edward Hancock and William Cullock:

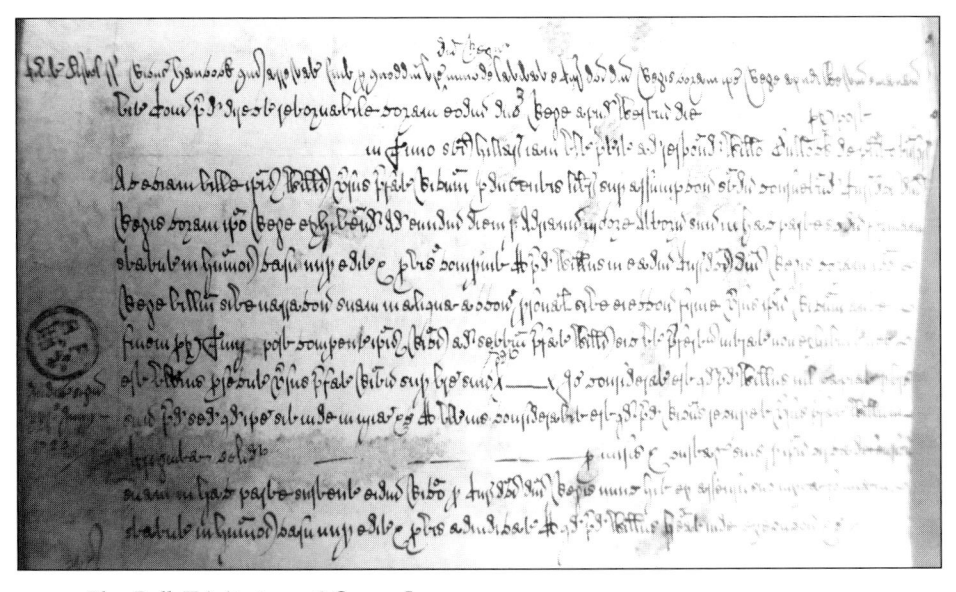

Plea Roll, Trinity term, 6 George I.

Example 2: Michaelmas term, 56 George III (1815)

In 1815, a dispute over monies owed, between John Rotten and Richard Bridges, was brought before the King's Bench.

The entry in the Index to Entry Book of Judgements (KB 168/182) provides the page number, 64 in the Entry Book of Judgements itself:

Bridges R^d)	19

The entry in the Entry Book of Judgements 1815 (KB 168/59 p.19) reads:

Mx	Jno Rotten	ats Richd Bridges for 700^l & ov^r	Jopson	–	2	B

The Docket Book, covering 1815, does not include any entry for Richard Bridges v John Rotten. There is no entry in the 1815 Warrant of Attorney to Confess Judgement (KB 128/185). These records were not always well kept, and this is not unusual.

The entry in the Plea Roll, Michaelmas term 56 George III, 1815 (KB 122/950 rot.65) provides details of Bridges' case against Rotten:

Michaelmas Term 56th George 3rd
Witness Edward Lord Ellenborough
    Middlesex to wit John Rotton puts in his place John Jopson his Attorney against Richard Bridges in a plea of Debt
    Middlesex to wit the said Richard Bridges puts in his place Thomas Wilson his attorney at the Suit of the said John Rotton in then plea aforesaid
    Middlesex to wit Be it remembered that on Monday next after the Morrow of all Souls in the same term before our Lord the King at Westminster comes John Rotton by John Jopson his attorney and brings into the said Court of our said Lord the King before the King himself now here his certain Bill against Richard Bridges being in the Custody of the Marshall of the Marshalsea of our Lord the now King before the King himself of a plea of Debt and there and pledges for the prosecution to with John Does and Richard Roe which said Bill follows in these Words to wit Middlesex to wit John Rotton

Insolvent Debtors – Court and Court Records

complains of Richard Bridges being in the Custody of the Marshall of the Marshalsea of our Lord the now King before the King himself of a plea that he render to the said John Rotton seven hundred Pounds of lawful money of Great Britain which he owes to and unjustly detains from him For that whereas the said Richard on the tenth day of November in the year of our Lord one thousand eight hundred and fifteen at Westminster in the County of Middlesex borrowed of the said John Rotton the said Seven hundred Pounds to be paid to the said John Rotton when he the said Richard should be thereto afterwards requested yet the said Richard (altho~ often requested &c) hath not yet paid the said seven hundred Pounds above demanded or any part thereof to the said John Rotton but he to pay the same or any part thereof hath hitherto wholly refused and still refuses to pay the said John Rotton his damage of Seven hundred pounds and therefore he brings his Suit &c

Plea And the said Richard by Thomas Wilson his Attorney comes and defends the Wrong and Injury when &c and says nothing in bar or preclusion of the said Action of the said John Rotton by which the said John Rotton remains there undefended against the said Richard

Therefore it is considered that the said John Rotton recover against the said Richard his said Debt and also eighty Shillings for his damages which he hath sustained as well by occasion of the detaining of the said Debt as for his Costs and Charges by him about his Suit in this behalf expended by the Courts of our Lord the King now here adjudged to the said John Rotton by his Assent and the said Richard in mercy &c. Judgement signed 15th Novr 1815

Exchequer of Pleas

Plea rolls	1236–1875	E 13
Bills and Writs	1260–1880	E 5
Docket books of judgements (to E 13/428-1322)	1603–11, 1625–56, 1669–1839	IND 1/4522-23, 4525-67
Chronological Calendars (to E 13/1-1245)	1272–1820	IND 1/7344-7363
Calendars (selective)	1293–1820	E 48
Repertory of Plea Rolls	1412–1499, 1559–1669, 1822–1830	E 14
Entry books of judgements (to E 13/1290-1469	1830–1875	IND 1/4243-4425
Indexes to Entry Books of Judgements [by Plaintiff]	1830–1875	IND 1/4426-4505

The records of the Exchequer are a rich source for the Tudor and Stuart periods, but less so for subsequent reigns.

The Court of Exchequer Plea Rolls, 1236–1875, E 13 are mainly filed by year until 1547, and thereafter mainly by term. At an early date the rolls ceased to record entries where the defendant failed to appear, which helped reduce the size of the rolls, but as a consequence does not reflect fully the larger number of suits that were brought, and which can only be identified where the files of Bills and Writs survive. The later rolls seem only to include enrolments of cases which reached judgement. Therefore, for all periods only a minority of suits resulted in entries in the Plea Rolls. The files of Bills and Writs (especially the Writs) offer a much fuller picture of the business of the court. The Plea Roll entries on Discovery are cross-references to both the Entry Books of Judgements and the Docket Books.

Insolvent Debtors – Court and Court Records

The Repertory of Plea Rolls, 1412–1499, 1559–1669, 1822–1830, E 14 reproduce in chronological order, for the same period, the marginal headings in the Plea Rolls, E 13.

Bills and Writs, 1260–1880, E 5 were to initiate suits. Writs were issued if the plaintiff was an accountant or debtor to the Crown, or other privileged party; and Bills were employed if the defendant was an accountant or debtor to the Crown, or other privileged party.

Other Series include: Docket Books of Judgements, 1603–1839 (gaps), IND 1 with entries on Discovery cross-refenced to the related Plea Roll; Entry Books of Judgements, 1830–1875, IND 1; also, various calendars and indexes, E 48 and IND 1.

EXAMPLE 1: TRINITY TERM, 25 GEORGE III (1785)

Mary Peerman's cause against John Hands was brought before the Exchequer Court in 1785. She claimed that the unpaid debt was the reason why she was then unable to settle her own debt to the Crown.

The Exchequer of Pleas Docket Book (IND 1/4538) refers to the case and provides the rotulus number on the Plea Roll, 43.

Hands	John of Harefield in the County of Middx	)	
	Gent. ats Mary Peerman Spinster	)	
	In Debt for £288 Money borrowed	)	43
	By Conf & 63. Dam~ Dax	)	

['ats' is an abbreviation for the words 'at suit of' and is used when the defendant files any pleadings; for instance, when the defendant enters a plea his name is put before that of the plaintiff, reversing the order in which they are normally recorded: John Hands (the defendant) at suit of Mary Peerman (the plaintiff).]

The Plea Roll for Trinity term, 25 Geo III, E 13/1106 furnishes the full details of Mary Peerman's case against John Hands and her liability to the Crown.

Pleas before the Barons of the Exchequer at Westminster among the Pleas of the Term of the Holy Trinity in Twenty fifth Year Reign of our Sovereign Lord George the Third By the Grace of God of Great Britain France and Ireland King Defender of the Faith and soforth.

Middlesex to wit Mary Peerman Spinster Debtor of his present Majesty comes before the Barons of this Exchequer at Westminster on the Fifteenth Day of June in this same Term by Elias White her Attorney and complains by Bill against John Hands of Harefield in the County of Middlesex Gentleman present here in Court the same Day Of a Plea that he render to the said Mary Two hundred and eighty eight Pounds of lawful Money of Great Britain which he owes to and unjustly detains from her For that Whereas the said John in the First Day of June in the Year of our Lord One thousand seven hundred and eighty five at Westminster in the said County of Middlesex had borrowed of the said Mary the aforesaid Sum of Two hundred and eighty eight Pounds to be paid to the said Mary when he the said John should be thereunto afterwards requested Yet the said John (although often thereto requested) the said Two hundred and eighty eight Pounds or any Part thereof to the said Mary hath not yet paid But to pay the same to the said Mary He the said John hath altogether hitherto refused and still refuses Wherefore the said Mary says that she is injured and hath sustained Damage to the Value of Twenty Pounds whereby she is the less able to satisfy his said Majesty the Debts which she owes him at his said Exchequer And therefore brings Suit &c Pledges to Prosecute John Doe and Richard Roe.

And the said John Hands by Edward Kinaston his Attorney comes and defends the Wrong and Injury when &c and prays the Hearing of the Bill aforesaid And it is read to him &c Which being read and heard the said John says that he cannot in any-wise deny the Action aforesaid of the said Mary nor but that he owes unto the said Mary the said Two hundred and eighty eight Pounds in Manner and Form as the said Mary hath above thereof declared against him Therefore

It is Considered by the Barons here that the said Mary do recover against the said John her Debt aforesaid And also her Damages by reason of detaining the said Debt to Sixty three Shillings to the said Mary with her Assent by the Court here Adjudged And the said John in Mercy &c

Judgmt signed 3d Octr 1785

EXAMPLE 2: MICHAELMAS TERM, 1 WILLIAM IV (1830)

For a second example from the first year of the reign of William IV, William Peckover v John Hume Long, there is considerably less surviving material.

The entry in Discovery for the Indexes to the Entry Books of Judgements, IND 1/4426 covering 1830 includes the reference for Entry Books themselves, IND 1:

> Index [by plaintiff] to IND 1/4243-IND 1/4246, entry books of judgment to Exchequer of Pleas: Plea Rolls.

In this case the Index to Entry Book of Judgements does not include any entry for the case. However, the Entry book of Judgments, IND 1/4243 does include the entry for William Peckover v John Hume Long:

12th Lincoln shire	Debt Conf^n	Wm Peckover old W^t atty debt Costs £	Jn° Hume Long 360	1	F Jeys	–	6	–	L

The Docket Book, IND 1/4552 also includes the entry for William Peckover v John Hume Long:

| Lincolnsh | Long | John Hume ats Wm Peckover Debt on Old War^t of Atty for £360 Costs £ F Jeys | 3 |

The Plea Roll itself, E 13/1288 does not include the entry for William Pickover v John Hume Long.

JOHN DOE AND RICHARD ROE
By the fourteenth century, 'John Doe' and 'Richard Roe' were already being used as substitute names on legal documents to protect the identities of the two witnesses needed for any legal action. 'Jane Doe' or 'Jane Roe' were also used for women. The names were also used when the person was unidentifiable, or on occasions were entirely fictitious: John Doe was the name given to a fictitious lessee of the plaintiff, in an action of eviction, the fictitious defendant being called Richard Roe.

This use of the names was mocked in the 1834 English song 'John Doe and Richard Roe':

Two giants live in Britain's land,
John Doe and Richard Roe,
Who always travel hand in hand,
John Doe and Richard Roe.
Their see-saw-sum's an ancient plan
To smell the purse of an Englishman,
And, 'ecod, they'll suck it all they can,
John Doe and Richard Roe,
No man yet ever spied
John Doe and Richard Roe
But they're giants, cannot be denied,
John Doe and Richard Roe.
…

> But, if a tradesman is in debt,
> John Doe and Richard Roe
> Undertake the cash to get,
> John Doe and Richard Roe.
> And, if he cannot raise the pelf,
> They send their bum to take the elf,
> For, if poor, they can seize Death himself,
> John Roe and Richard Roe.
> The bum doth to the poor man say, –
> John Doe and Richard Roe
> Desire that you come to-day
> To John Doe and Richard Roe.
> He tries to give the bum leg-bail,
> But, 'lack, it is of no avail,
> He's sure to get locked up in jail
> By John Doe and Richard Roe.

EQUITY COURTS
Court of Requests

Court of Requests: Process Books including Orders, Decrees and Affidavits	Aug 1492–Mar 1642	REQ 1
Court of Requests: Pleadings	Aug 1485- Jan 1649	REQ 2

Records of judgements, court orders, process books and other administrative records, REQ 1, have survived reasonably well, but many have yet to be sorted and are difficult to identify. TNA's Research Guide, *Court of Requests records 1485–1642* provides some information on how to identify many of the available records.

A similar situation exists with the records of Pleadings, REQ 2: over half the cases (including half of those dating from the reign of James I and all from Charles I) have not been indexed or catalogued in any way. The situation for records of proceedings created during and between the reigns of Henry VII and Elizabeth I, and around half the proceedings from the reign of James I, is slightly better. TNA's Research Guide is again a great help.

Pleadings, 1585–1587, REQ 2/1-15, can be searched by keyword on Discovery. The period 1547–1625 is indexed in *Lists and Indexes No.21; List of Proceedings in the Court of Requests preserved in the Public Record Office. Vol. 1* and *Lists and Indexes, Supplementary series; No. 7, Vols. 1,2,3,4.*

EXAMPLE: 39 ELIZABETH I (1597)
Lists and Indexes No.21; List of Proceedings in the Court of Requests preserved in the Public Record Office. Vol.1 includes reference to a case of debt involving Joan Conyers of Northumberland, 'Bundle CXXVI – No. 6' – viz. REQ 2/126 No.6:

		BUNDLE CXXVI.		
6	Joan Conyers	John Flemyng	Debt	Northumb.

Several documents survive in the Proceedings, REQ 2/126 in Bundle 6 including Joan (Johan) Conyers' original complaint:

> To the Quenes most excellent maiestie
> In most humble wise compleyning sheweth and besecheth your highness your poore and dailie Orartice Johan Conyers late wife of Gregory Conyers late one of the Gonners of Barwick deceased where John Flemyng nowe serving in Barwick in the office of Mr Gunner there was indebted and did owe unto your poore Oratrice for wages due to her said late husband and for victualls lent monney and other thinges amounting to tenne poundes eighteen shillings As by a bill of parcells thereof reddye to be shewed it dothe and maye appeare And albeit that your said Oratrice hath many tymes gentlie required the same yet he hath refused & still doth refuse to paye the same, denyenge that he did owe anye suche debt, And forasmuche as the same John Flemyng doth well

knowe thinking thereby to delaye your poor Oratrice of her said debte to the greate hindrance of the same your Oratrice, In considerac~on whereof it maye please your matie of youre accustomed goodness to graunt your maties comyssion to be directed out of the co~te of requests unto Mr Anthony Adderson maior of Barwicke Sr Will~m Drury knight highe Marshall Sr Vallentyne Browne Treasurer of Barwick Mr John Lovell gentleman porter & Mr James Meares freman authorising them thereby to heare & examine the premysses and to call before them Symon Bugar the Mr mate of the greate orden~ce at Barwicke Will~m Larking one of the gunners perteyninge to the great orden~ce and John Leeche one other of the gunners perteyninge to the said greate orden~ce whoe canne thestefieth the truthe and of the circu~stances thereof and thereupon to take suche order therein as to their wisdomes and discrec~ons shall seme to stande with equitie and good conscience And she shall daylie praye for your most noble and Royall estate longe to contynue.

Court of Star Chamber

Proceedings	1485–1509	STAC 1
Proceedings	c.1450–1625	STAC 2
Proceedings	Hen VII–Eliz I	STAC 3
Proceedings	Hen VII–Eliz I	STAC 4
Proceedings	1558–1601	STAC 5
Proceedings	1558–1601	STAC 7
Proceedings	1601–1625	STAC 8
Proceedings	1625–1641	STAC 9

The proceedings, recorded in English, include all the details of a case as presented by both plaintiff and defendant. These therefore could include the plaintiff's original bill of complaint, the defendant's response, any counter-arguments from the plaintiff and/or the defendant, and questions put to, and answers from, any witnesses.

STAC 1–STAC 4, STAC 7 and STAC 9 are searchable on Discovery by plaintiff, defendant subject, place and county. STAC 5 is searchable by first plaintiff and first defendant only. STAC 8 by plaintiff, defendant, subject and county.

Example: 16 James I (1618)
There is a detailed description on Discovery of the cause brought by Alice Harris against William Beamont and his son, William:

> Plaintiffs: Alice Harris, late wife of William Harris, yeoman.
> Defendants: William Beamont and William Beamont his son, masons.
> Subject: Perjury in action for debts incurred by the said William Harris for building at Belchalwell, etc.
> Dorset. November 1618

The surviving documents comprise Alice Harris's Bill of Complaint and the Answer from William Beaumont and his son William. Both are lengthy documents containing very detailed information about the case.

PALACE COURT
The Bail Books, 1691–1836, PALA 1 give the names of the parties to actions, with details of the bailsmen – often these are the fictitious John Doe and Richard Roe. The volumes for 1778–1836 have internal indexes to defendants. There are a few gaps between 1692 and 1773, not all of which are clear from the catalogue.

The Custody Books, 1754–1842, PALA 2 are indexed by plaintiff. Each entry gives the name of the person committed, the date they

Insolvent Debtors – Court and Court Records

Bail Books (Some gaps before 1773. Internal indexes 1778–1836)	1691–1836	PALA 1
Custody Books	1754–1842	PALA 2
Docket Books	1802–1849	PALA 3
Habeas Corpus Books	1700–1849	PALA 4
Plaint Books	1686–1849	PALA 5
Plea Books	1629–1849	PALA 6
Miscellanea	1630–1850	PALA 9

were brought into custody, the warrant for their arrest (usually the date of a writ and for whom it was issued, although surrenders in discharge of bail are also common), and the sum involved. They are usually also annotated with the date of discharge.

The Docket Books, 1802–1849, PALA 3 also name the parties concerned and record the verdicts of the court; they have an internal index to plaintiffs for the whole period. Included is the number of the rotulus of the Plea Roll, PALA 6, on which it is enrolled.

The Habeas Corpus Books, 1700–1849, PALA 4 are indexed by defendant with each entry signed by the defendant's attorney or his clerk. The amount of the debt involved is also noted.

Plaint Books, 1886–1849, PALA 5 briefly record all actions or plaints brought to the Palace Court, noting the name of the person making the plaint, the person against whom it was made, the type of case (usually debt), and the sum involved. Many of the debts mentioned are of 99 shillings, to ensure that the sum fell under £5 and so could not be removed to a superior court by the defendant under a writ of *habeas corpus*, although much larger sums also regularly appear. Again, some of the headings note that the pledges for prosecution of a suit were the fictitious John Doe and Richard Roe.

The earlier part of the Series of Plea Books, 1629–1849, PALA 6 has many gaps which, because they are so numerous, are not pointed out in the catalogue. The Series is complete only from 1793. Entries in the rolls for cases which reached judgment from 1802 can be found through the docket books in PALA 3. In addition, some bail books in PALA 1 include cross-references to the rolls.

Miscellaneous records of the Palace Court, PALA 9, include judges' notebooks, attorneys' transcripts, documents concerning the appointment to and surrender of court offices, material about prisoners committed to the Marshalsea Prison, account books, exhibits and a few posters and handbills.

EXAMPLE: 56 GEORGE III (1815)

In May 1815, Joseph Taylor the elder and Joseph Naylor the younger took Richard Cresswell to court claiming they were owed £14.0.0 for goods supplied.

The Bail Book 5 Jan 1815 – 24 Dec 1818 (PALA 1/60) shows the names, addresses and occupations of those who stood surety:

		Court held on Friday 19th May 1815		
W	Richard Cresswell ats Joseph Taylor the elder and Joseph Taylor the younger	the like [bailed by John Doe and Richard Roe]	A	John Hanscombe ats Robert Taylor

In the Plea Book, (PALA 6/98) the plaintiffs are recorded as Naylor rather than Taylor:

1815
The Court of the Kings
Palace of Westminster, June 30th 1815

Joseph Naylor the elder and Joseph Naylor the younger by William Railton their attorney complain of Richard Creswell in a plea of trespass on the case For that whereas the said Richard Naylor & ors heretofore to wit on the Twenty fourth

Insolvent Debtors – Court and Court Records

day of April in the Year of our Lord a one thousand eight hundred and fifteen at Westminster in the County of Cresswell Middlesex and within the jurisdiction of this Court was indebted to the said Joseph the elder and Joseph the younger in the sum of Fourteen Pounds of lawful money of the United Kingdom of Great Britain and Ireland Current in England for divers Goods Wares and Merchandize of the said Joseph the elder and Joseph the younger before that time sold and delivered to the said Richard at his special instance and request And being so indebted he the said Richard in consideration thereof afterwards to wit on the same day and year aforesaid at Westminster aforesaid in the County and jurisdiction aforesaid undertook and then and there faithfully promised the said Joseph the elder and Joseph the younger to pay the said sum of Fourteen pounds whenever afterwards he the said Richard should be thereunto requested And which also afterwards to wit on the same day and year aforesaid at Westminster aforesaid in the County and Jurisdiction aforesaid in consideration that the said Joseph the elder and Joseph the younger at the like special instance and request of the said Richard had before that time there sold and delivered to him the said Richard divers other Goods wares and Merchandize of them the said Joseph the elder and Joseph the younger [etc].

PALATINATE OF LANCASTER COURT OF COMMON PLEAS

Plea Rolls	1400–1848	PL 15
Dockets	1377–1869	PL 16
Writ Files	1434–1846	PL 20
Sessional Papers	HEN VIII–1848	PL 21
Declaration Files and Indexes	1788–1874	PL 22
Miscellaneous Records	1518–1875	PL 24

Records of the Palatinate of Lancaster's Court of Common Pleas relating to common law jurisdiction include several Series.

Plea Rolls are in PL 15. These mainly include cases of trespass, debt and land, and include pleadings, judgments, writs of process, recognizances and other material. The Docket Rolls and Books in PL 16 record the progress in pleas, fines and recoveries dealt with by the court for which action was recorded on the Plea Rolls. They usually cite the membrane number of the Plea Roll.

Many Writs in PL 20 include a cross-reference to the plea roll on which proceedings in the case were recorded.

Files of sessional papers are in PL 21; declarations, formerly on those files, were kept in a separate Series from 1788 in PL 22. Most of the actions, tried at twice-yearly sessions (Lent or Summer), concern trespass, ejectment and, above all, debt.

Miscellaneous administrative records of the Prothonotary are in PL 24.

EXAMPLE: LENT TERM, 40 GEORGE III (1800)

George Robinson brought an action against John Grantham, a butcher from Manchester, complaining that he was owed £40. The entry in the Plea Roll commences, and ends, as follows:

> Lancashire To Wit John Grantham late of Manchester in the said County Butcher was attached to answer George Robinson of a Plea of Trespass upon the Case and so forth and whereupon the Said George by John Ainsworth his Attorney complains That Whereas the said John Grantham the first day of March in the year of our Lord one thousand eight hundred at Preston in the said County was indebted to the said George in forty pounds of lawful Money of Great Britain for so much Money by the said George to and for the use of the said John Grantham […]
>
> And the said John Grantham by Edward Lodge his Attorney cometh and defendeth the force and injury when &c

Insolvent Debtors – Court and Court Records

and saith that he did not undertake and promise in manner and form as the said George hath above thereof complained against him and of this he putteth himself upon the Country &c and the said George doth so likewise Therefore the Sheriff of the County aforesaid is commanded that he cause to come her at Lancaster the first day of the next General Session of the Assize here to be holden twelve &c by whom &c and who neither &c recognize &c because as well &c.

Chapter 5

INSOLVENT DEBTORS – IMPRISONMENT

Throughout Britain there were prisons where debtors were incarcerated. As has been seen, debtors came under the jurisdiction of different courts of law to those of common criminals or felons and, before the nineteenth century, most prisons were administered locally with central government having no real responsibility for them.

Prison as a punishment only began to take hold in the late eighteenth century. The main exception to this was the imprisonment of debtors, a concept that dated back to the thirteenth century. The assumption had been that the threat of prison would act as a deterrent: if a person was owed money, and it had not been repaid, then the thought of imprisonment would encourage him to pay up.

Most local prisons had their own wings or separate quarters where debtors were housed. The separation of debtors from other prisoners was formalized by legislation passed in 1670. In some towns there were separate prisons for debtors. Alternatively, many were sent from different parts of the country, especially from the home counties, to one of the debtors' prisons in London.

Release only came when the debt was paid off, either from money earned while in prison, or if friends or relations raised the amount owing. However, as much of their keep had to be paid for by the prisoners themselves, until the law changed in 1815 many debtors

Insolvent Debtors – Imprisonment

found themselves worse off after a few years in prison than when they arrived. The small amounts they could earn were rarely sufficient to cover their keep.

A prisoner's comfort, or otherwise, while incarcerated was dependent on their affluence – which, being debtors, was presumably negligible – or, more often, on the generosity of friends and family.

In 1850 William Hepworth Dixon voiced a commonly held, sympathetic view when he wrote:

> The area is filled with men and women – many of them honest, and all unfortunate. No one here has but a sad tale to tell. The world has gone wrong with all of them; but hope has not yet left their perturbed hearts.

Debtors' prisons varied in the amount of freedom they allowed those imprisoned for debt and usually there were not the harsh punitive rules there were in the rest of the prison. Although prison life was usually more relaxed for debtors than for criminals, they nevertheless had to adhere to certain regulations: they had to clean their cells, passages, staircases, day-rooms, yards, furniture and utensils. They were also expected to attend divine service.

Debtors did not suffer the same automatic loss of status and reputation as other convicts and were allowed extensive privileges compared to other prisoners, which included being allowed visitors, and providing their own food and clothing. They were locked up at night and unlocked in the morning. Many debtors had their wives and children living with them, in a desperate attempt to avoid the workhouse. Often any rules were applied loosely, and many debtors enjoyed exceptional freedoms during their incarceration.

In fact, depending on how much money you had at your disposal to pay the Marshal (as the jailer was known in some prisons), it was possible to live a perfectly comfortable life as an inmate. You could buy anything from fine furnishings for your room to a haircut. Even a day off could be purchased from the Marshal. A 'liberty ticket' entitled you to absent yourself for up to three days.

On the other hand, prisoners were subjected to a raft of fees once they were imprisoned. They had to pay fees on admission and discharge, as well as room rents while residing there – the more expensive the room, the better the conditions. The jailer raised his income directly from the prisoners, for renting a room, for food and drink, and for clothes and bedding.

The following table shows the rates and fees charged in 1774 for debtors in the Sheriff's Ward at the Devon County Prison for Debtors:

	£.	s.	d.
For the commitment fee of every prisoner for debt, damages and contempts though it be on several actions or processes only	0	13	4
To the Turnkey	0	1	0
For every liberate	0	2	0
For the use of a bed in a single room for one person by the week	0	3	0
The use of a room where there are two or more beds and two lodge in a bed each person by the week	0	1	3
The use of the common room if the keeper finds bedding for each person by the week	0	1	0
If the prisoner finds bedding	nothing		

At most debtors' prisons, there was a market where food could be bought. If any debtors were too poor to provide for themselves, they were entitled to a weekly county allowance. In 1841, the *Sixth report of the Inspectors of Prisons of Great Britain* stated that at Lancaster Castle, the county allowance for debtors was:

> 7 lbs. of bread, 2 lbs. of meat, 10 lbs. of potatoes, and 4½ oz. of salt, to which ½ a lb. of cheese and 4 herrings weekly were added from a charity fund.

Insolvent Debtors – Imprisonment

Prisoners could save on room fees by sharing with other inmates. Such conditions inevitably led to ill-health. James Grant in his *Sketches in London*, written in 1838, commented:

> The anxiety of the poorer class of prisoner to save a few shillings per week, by congregating together in one room, has often led to six or eight persons vegetating together in a dark, dirty apartment, measuring only sixteen by nineteen feet.

Gambling or games of any description were supposed to be strictly prohibited, but this was not always the case. On visiting the debtors' prison at Lancaster Castle in 1847, one inspector complained:

The Rake's Progress, plate 4, *'Arrested for Debt as Going to Court'. From the original picture by William Hogarth, engraved by H. Adlard, published by Jones & Co.*

> Instead of being a place of rigid economy and other reflection, [it] is like a somewhat noisy tavern and tea-garden: the prisoners idling about, smoking, drinking, talking in a loud voice, and playing at skittles and pitch-farthing.

Local prisons (and particularly debtors' prisons, which ironically tended to have a rather higher class of inmate) were, before 1878, privately run, self-financing, profit-making enterprises.

The prisons had very few staff. Given such circumstances, there was little control over what went on inside the prison, their only role being to prevent escapes. The prisoners themselves more or less regulated life inside the gaols. To a great extent, the debtors' prisons were private enterprises. Elected bodies of inmates tried to keep order and arbitrate quarrels, supervised the letting of rooms, arranged cleaning, and even enforced weights and measures in the shops.

Whereas many debtors may have had it 'easy' in prison, others certainly did not; and neither did the family left abandoned. In a lengthy article in *The Idler* in January 1759 the argument against the imprisonment of debtors was forcibly made:

> A debtor is dragged to prison, pitied for a moment, and then forgotten; another follows him, and is lost alike in the caverns of oblivion; but when the whole mass of calamity rises up at once, when twenty thousand reasonable beings are heard all groaning in unnecessary misery, not by the infirmity of nature, but the mistake or negligence of policy, who can forbear to pity and lament, to wonder and abhor?
>
> There is here no need of declamatory vehemence; we live in an age of commerce and computation; let us therefore coolly enquire what is the sum of evil which the imprisonment of debtors brings upon our country.
>
> It seems to be the opinion of the later computists, that the inhabitants of England do not exceed six millions, of which

twenty thousand is the three hundredth part. What shall we say of the humanity or the wisdom of a nation, that voluntarily sacrifices one in every three hundred to lingering destruction?

The misfortunes of an individual do not extend their influence to many; yet, if we consider the effects of consanguinity and friendship, and the general reciprocation of wants and benefits, which make one man dear or necessary to another, it may reasonably be supposed, that every man languishing in prison gives trouble of some kind to two others who love or need him. By this multiplication of misery we see distress extended to the hundredth part of the whole society. If we estimate at a shilling a day what is lost by the inaction and consumed in the support of each man thus chained down to involuntary idleness, the public loss will rise in one year to three hundred thousand pounds; in ten years to more than a sixth part of our circulating coin.

As corruption within debtors' prisons reached absurd levels, it was realized that things had to change. John Howard (1726–1790), High Sheriff of Bedfordshire, was a political reformer whose campaigning included the abolition of gaolers' fees and improvement in prison hygiene and prisoners' health. In 1777 he published *The State of the Prisons in England, and An Account of the Principal Lazarettos of Europe*, which provided details of all the prisons he had visited in person. Howard's campaigning led to the passing of the 1774 Gaol Act, which abolished gaolers' fees and provided for the improvement in conditions for prisoners. However, the Act was mostly ignored by the gaolers and it was not until 1815 that gaolers were finally banned from charging prisoners.

In the eighteenth century, by a writ of *habeas corpus*, debtors were allowed to move from one debtors' prison to another. In some extreme circumstances, prisoners chose to take advantage of this arrangement by choosing one prison as their winter residence and one as their summer home.

In 1847, new instructions were sent to all prisons in Britain ensuring that those owing small sums of money would get better treatment, and thenceforth they would not have to share cells with serious debtors or criminals. The official direction stated 'they shall as far as the construction of the prison allow thereof, be separated from other debtors, but shall not be placed in separate confinement, or with any class of criminal prisoners'. This was the start of a more considerate attitude to debtors, which would eventually result in the ending of imprisonment for debt.

It eventually became obvious that imprisoning people for debt was pointless. The nineteenth century brought further reforms and finally an end to the notorious London debtors' prisons. Periodic Acts of Parliament (37 between 1670 and 1800) for the Relief of Insolvent Debtors allowed the release of debtors from prison if they applied to a Justice of the Peace and submitted a schedule of their assets (see Chapter 3). Eventually, the Debtors' Act of 1869 abolished imprisonment for debt, although debtors who had the means to pay their debt, but refused to do so, could still be incarcerated for up to six weeks.

Chapter 6

INSOLVENT DEBTORS – COMMON LAW AND CENTRAL PRISONS AND PRISON RECORDS

By 1800, there were at least nine specialist debtors' prisons in London. The majority of debtors, especially those convicted at one of the three common law or other central courts, found themselves in one of the five major London gaols: the King's Bench, the Fleet, the Marshalsea, Horsemonger Lane (Surrey County Gaol) or, from 1815, in Whitecross Street Prison. These were the Crown (government) prisons attached to the courts in which debtors were condemned to imprisonment. The Fleet Prison, for example, received people judged by the Court of Chancery, while the King's Bench Prison accepted prisoners from the King's Bench, and so on – although there were always exceptions to the general rule.

The prisons differed in their construction and the way they were run. In his 1850 book, *The London Prisons*, William Hepworth Dixon wrote:

> Whitecross Street is entirely a debtors' prison. It has never been a place for criminals, and consequently it presents a totally different aspect to the eye. This is observable in the character of the building, as well as in the character of its inmates.

Although the majority of debtors spent a reasonably short time in prison – less than six months – some were imprisoned for considerable lengths of time: in 1844, forty-nine prisoners had been in the Queen's Bench Prison for more than three years and of these seven had been imprisoned in the 1820s and one in 1812.

The population of debtors' prisons was at times substantial. In 1790, 1,200 people were sent to jail for debt in London and Middlesex alone. In 1826, on one specific day there were 2,861 people in debtors' prisons, of whom 1,737 were in the four main London prisons. By 1844, the total number had risen to 2,154.

The Times reported in 1840:

> A recent return was made by Mr Barratt, the keeper of Whitecross-street Prison, of the number of persons [debtors] in his custody, as ordered by the House of Lords … In the Queen's Bench Prison there is a person name York who has been located within the walls upwards of 18 years; and in the Fleet a man named Board has been domiciled upwards of 20 years. These persons could have petitioned the Insolvent Debtor's Court any time after they went to prison.

Many of the prisons had two sides: the Master's Side and the Common or Poor Side. Common Side prisoners were those without means who were provided with free accommodation and were eligible for a statutory weekly payment, as well as other money received from local and national charities. The Master's Side was usually far larger: for instance, the King's Bench Prison had twenty-four Common Side rooms and eighty-four Master's Side rooms, which could be rented by the better-off prisoners. In the 1800s, they could expect to pay a weekly rent of half-a-crown for this slightly-more-comfortable accommodation, although it could never be described as lavish. The King's Bench Prison even had a separate 'State House'.

Other rooms cost one shilling a week and inmates were expected to provide their own furniture. Poorer inmates, however, had to share rooms, sleep two to a bed, or even in the chapel or on benches in the 'Tap'. If two people had to share the same room, they were only charged sixpence each, and if there were three people sharing the fee was fourpence each.

If a new arrival was to share a room, he was said to be 'chummed' on the original occupant. When the newcomer arrived, he was issued with a 'chum ticket'. On the ticket was written, by an officer of the prison (or 'chum-master'), the name of the prisoner and the number of the room he had been allocated. The existing occupant either had to share the apartment with him or pay him five shillings to 'purchase him out'. This he had to accept and therefore was forced to find an alternative room to share.

When the prison was overcrowded, the inmates already in situ might have had two persons 'chummed' on them, which meant that if they wanted to live alone they had to pay ten shillings a week to these 'chums', plus another shilling in rent to the Warden. Until an Act of Parliament prohibited the 'chumming' of more than two individuals on an inmate as many as three people could be 'chummed' on an individual who previously had sole tenancy of a room. In some circumstances the chum-master billeted a newcomer, who wanted a more comfortable room and was willing to sacrifice the five shillings 'purchase out' fee, with an inmate prepared to share his room with a person of the same social rank as himself.

It was not unknown for a long-term prisoner to decorate and furnish his rooms and then let them out to any new prisoner who could afford to pay the rent demanded. As much as a guinea a week was known to have been charged, the 'landlord' then sharing a room elsewhere at a considerably lower rent.

Inmates could buy their own food at the prison bakehouse, have refreshments in the coffee-house (open to the public) or indulge in the strong beer in the 'Tap'. The King's Bench also had its own post office.

The King's Bench, Fleet and Marshalsea all had taprooms (the 'Tap') for the sale of beer and wine. Beer was often a thorny subject: in 1771 the prisoners in the King's Bench destroyed over fifty barrels

'A Whistling Shop. Tom and Jerry visiting Logic on board the Fleet'. Drawn and engraved by I.R. & G. Cruikshank. Published in Life in London *by Pierce Egan (Sherwood, Jones & Co., 1821).*

of beer claiming it had been watered. The sale of spirits was banned in prisons, but this did not stop gin and brandy being obtained locally.

Prisoners could earn money by working: jobs were available cleaning and maintaining the prison. Many continued pursuing their own trades. The prison authorities tolerated such activities. In 1815, the Marshal of the King's Bench noted only one restriction: 'we do not allow joiners to have any, large pieces of timber'. As an illustration, in 1782, Harriott Hart had a business making feather hats in the Marshalsea.

Prisoners could even have their families stay with them. While touring the English prisons in 1776, John Howard counted 242 debtors in the Fleet Prison, with 475 wives and children between them. Others made money by running illegal 'whistling shops' for the sale of spirits.

Insolvent Debtors – Common Law and Central Prisons and Records

Whitecross Street introduced a new regime and was more restrictive than the other major gaols. Prisoners slept in dormitories and were locked up early in the evenings, and visiting hours were limited. However, enterprising debtors found it easy to be transferred to the more liberal King's Bench.

Inmates did not have to actually live inside the Fleet. In return for a fee they were permitted to take lodgings within a designated area outside the prison, bounded by the Old Bailey, Fleet Street, Ludgate Hill and Farringdon Street, embracing a circumference of three miles. This was known as the 'Liberty of the Fleet' or the 'Rule of the Fleet'. By the fourteenth century payment for this privilege was made to the Warden and was based on a percentage of the debt owed by the prisoner – never exceeding 5 per cent on the first £100 or 2½ per cent on the second. Similar arrangements existed at the Marshalsea and King's Bench prisons.

Permissions to exit the prison on a daily basis were called 'day rules'. Application was made to the Warden, to whom yet another fee was payable. The system was described by James Grant in his *Sketches in London*, written in 1838:

> Day rules may be had any day, during term, on which the Courts of Common Pleas and Exchequer respectively sit, on applying to the Warden, and furnishing the same kind of security as in the case just mentioned. A day rule enables the prisoner to go at large during the particular day for which it is granted, from the opening of the prison gates in the morning till eleven o clock at night. The expenses of a day rule, exclusive, of course, of the amount of security required, are four shillings and sixpence. Of this sum the Warden gets one shilling; the clerk of the papers one shilling and tenpence; and the officers of the court, who grant the rules, receive the remaining one shilling and eight-pence.

The Fleet and Marshalsea prisons were abolished from 31 May 1842 and the Queen's Bench Prison, renamed the Queen's Prison, became the only one for all debtors, bankrupts and other persons who might previously have been imprisoned in any of the three prisons. The Queen's Prison eventually closed in 1862.

The Marshalsea was up for sale in 1843 and the Fleet finally closed in 1846. Whitecross Street Prison was closed soon after imprisonment for debt was abolished in 1869. Today nothing remains of the Fleet, King's Bench or Whitecross Street prisons. Meagre remnants of the Marshalsea are still to be found in Southwark.

THE GORDON RIOTS

Burning of Newgate Prison during the Gordon Riots. Published in Old and New London *Vol.2 (Cassell, Petter & Galpin, 1878).*

The Gordon Riots of 1780 began as an anti-Catholic protest in London against the Papists Act of 1778. The Act had been intended to reduce official discrimination against British Catholics. This idea of tolerating Catholics was deeply resented in Protestant

Insolvent Debtors – Common Law and Central Prisons and Records

England. The fuse was lit in 1780, when Lord George Gordon called for the repeal of the Catholic Relief Act of 1778 and a return to the repression of Catholics.

On 2 June Gordon led a crowd of 60,000 to the House of Commons to present a petition stating that the legislation encouraged 'popery' and was a threat to the Church of England. Protests were violent and aimed at Catholic targets, such as homes and chapels, even a distillery owned by a Catholic in High Holborn. Events descended into chaos. Members of the Commons and Lords were met with a barrage of abuse and physical violence, with the crowd only successfully dispersed once troops were called to the scene. For a week thereafter, violence raged across the capital and was the most destructive in the history of London thus far.

The Gordon Riots resulted in the destruction of at least eight London prisons and houses of correction: Newgate, the Fleet, Clerkenwell House of Correction, New Prison, Surrey House of Correction, the Clink, King's Bench Prison and the Borough Compter. The rioters also seem to have expressed a more general frustration: the Bank of England came under attack and prisoners were released from London's principal prisons. 15,000 troops poured into London to quell the disturbances and nearly 300 rioters were shot dead by soldiers.

Painted on the wall of Newgate prison was the proclamation that the inmates had been freed by the authority of 'His Majesty, King Mob'. The term 'King Mob' was afterwards used to denote an unruly and fearsome proletariat.

All but the Clink were immediately rebuilt, with few changes to the design of the original buildings, reflecting both the urgency with which the reconstruction was required and the fundamentally pragmatic approach of most magistrates.

The 1781 Destruction of Prisons by Rioters Act specified that keepers whose prisons had been affected by the riots should submit a list of all prisoners in custody on 1 January 1781, as well as a list of those who had escaped.

Farringdon Street and the Fleet Prison. Published in London and its Environs in the Nineteenth Century *(Jones & Co., London, 1829).*

FLEET PRISON

The Fleet was the first purpose-built house of correction in London, becoming infamous as a den of vice and immorality. It was constructed in the twelfth century on the east side of Farringdon Street, just beyond the city walls, taking its name from the nearby Fleet river. From the Middle Ages onwards, the ancient Fleet Prison served as a prison for debtors and bankrupts and for persons charged with contempt. It was during the late seventeenth and early eighteenth century that the Fleet gained notoriety as a debtors' prison, holding anyone under the process of debt issued by either the Court of Common Pleas or the Court of Exchequer – or for the confinement of parties who had been found guilty of contempt of either of these courts – or committed from the Court of Star Chamber or the Palatinate of Lancaster Court of Common Pleas.

The Fleet Prison was destroyed three times, once in the Peasants'

Insolvent Debtors – Common Law and Central Prisons and Records

Revolt in 1381, then later during the Great Fire of London in 1666 and again in the Gordon Riots of 1780. Each time it was rebuilt in a similar style, with several long buildings, consisting of four upper storeys and a cellar, arranged around inner yards where the more active prisoners would play tennis, fives, skittles or racquets.

Set into the outside walls of the Fleet Prison, bordering Farringdon Street, was an iron cage, the begging grate, behind which an impecunious inmate would sit rattling a money box, exclaiming, according to Dickens, 'Pray remember the poor debtors, pray remember the poor debtor'.

The National Archives has an account book for the Fleet begging grate from 1822–1829. This lists the beggars and the paltry sums they collected, as well as donations from institutions. On 17 December

'The begging grate at the Fleet Street Prison', by Thomas Hosmer Shepherd, early nineteenth century.

1822, Robert Beldon collected eightpence and James Conner got elevenpence the following day, while on Christmas Day William Telling collected a more substantial three shillings and ninepence.

| Begging Grate Book | 1822–29 | PRIS 10/6 |

Institutions, such as the City Livery Companies and St Thomas's Hospital, also occasionally made donations to help the poorest inmates. The Begging Grate Book includes many references to such donations. In December 1822, the Leather Sellers' Company contributed six shillings plus two shillings worth of bread, and the Court of Chancery contributed five guineas.

John Howard in his 1776 report on the Fleet commented:

> They also play in the yard at skittles, mississippi, fives, tennis, &c. And not only Prisoners: I saw among them several butchers and others from the market; who are admitted here as at another public house. The same may be seen in other Prisons where the Gaoler keeps or lets the tap. Besides the inconvenience of this to Prisoners; the frequenting a Prison lessens the dread of being confined in one.
>
> On Monday night there is a Wine-Club: on Thursday night a Beer-Club: each lasting usually till one or two in the morning. I need not say how much riot these occasion; and how the sober Prisoners are annoyed by them.

Both the Fleet and the King's Bench prisons allowed prisoners to live outside the walls. The Fleet had an area surrounding the prison about a mile and a quarter in circumference, called the Liberty. Prisoners who could provide security and pay off part of their debt could live there. There was a similar arrangement around the King's Bench called the Rules. In 1776, about a third of prisoners lived outside the King's Bench.

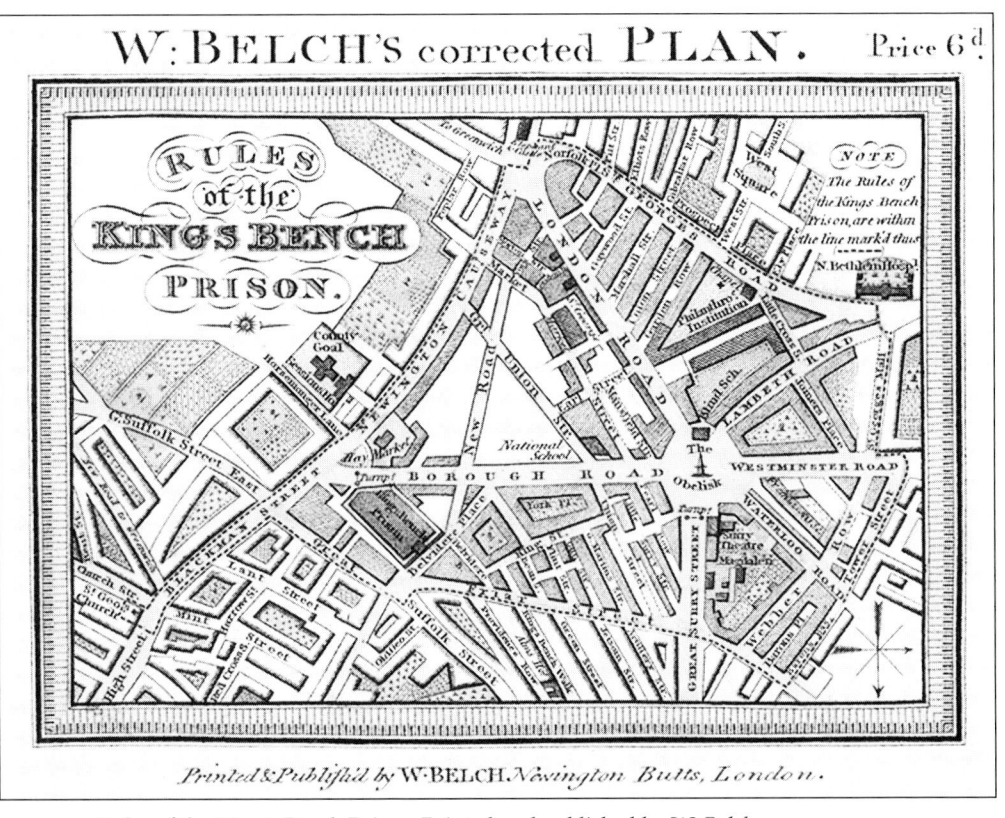

Rules of the King's Bench Prison. Printed and published by W. Belch.

James Grant, in his 1838 *Sketches in London*, wrote:

> There is a certain space without the (Fleet) prison, which is called 'The Rule'. Within this space the prisoners are permitted to reside at large, on furnishing satisfactory security against their escape. This is done by a warrant of attorney to confess judgment, and on paying the Warden of the prison a certain percentage upon the debt, the amount of which percentage varies according to the magnitude of the debt ... The space within the rules embraces a circumference of three miles and includes the London Coffee House.

'Interior of the Fleet Prison – the Racquet Court'. Published in Old and New London, *Vol. 2 (Cassell, Petter & Galpin, 1878).*

Not only was the Fleet cleaner and better run than the King's Bench, it also had a further advantage: persons living within the Rules had access to the London Coffee House and the Belle Sauvage public house.

However, Dickens painted a grim picture of the conditions at the Fleet Prison. When Mr Pickwick arrived, he was shown 'a dark and filthy staircase, which appeared to lead to a range of damp and gloomy stone vaults, beneath the ground'. '"And there I suppose are the little cellars where the prisoners keep their coals." He said'. However, these were the cells for the poorest inmates, called ironically Bartholomew Fair.

The state of the Fleet is light-heartedly brought to life in an extract from a poem, 'The Humours of the Fleet', written by a debtor in 1749:

> Such the amusement of this merry jail
> Which you'll not reach, if friends or money fail
> For ere its three-fold gates it will unfold
> The destined captive must produce some gold;
> Four guineas at the least for different fees
> Completes your Habeas, and commands the keys;
> Which done and safely in, no more you're bled
> If you have cash, you'll find a friend and bed;
> But that deficient, you'll but ill betide
> Lie in the hall, perhaps, or common side.

FLEET MARRIAGES

The Fleet had a chapel and a chaplain to serve the inmates. Regular marriages were conducted there, but over time the chapel became London's centre for clandestine marriages.

The Marriage Duty Acts of 1694 and 1695 required that places 'pretending to be exempt from the visitation of the Bishop' should only conduct marriages by banns or licence. Clergymen who ignored the order were liable to a fine of £100. The number of irregular marriages generally decreased, but business for those clergy who had little to lose, such as those imprisoned for debt or those without benefice, increased. In 1696, An Act for the enforcing the Laws which restrain Marriages without Licence or Banns had noted that, 'divers ministers, being in prison for debt and otherwise, do marry in the said prisons, many persons resorting thither for the purposes aforesaid, and in other places for lucre and gain to themselves'.

The Fleet was, or at least claimed to be, outside the jurisdiction of the church authorities. Clandestine marriage in the Fleet chapel flourished. Anyone could visit the prison and its inmates,

'A Wedding in the Fleet': from an eighteenth-century print. Published in Old and New London *Vol.2 (Cassell, Petter & Galpin, 1878).*

including those clergymen who were willing to marry anyone, for a fee, without asking too many questions. In 1711, a fine was introduced on prison keepers who permitted marriage in prison chapels without banns or licences.

The result was that the clandestine marriage market simply moved outside the prison walls. Many inmates lived in the Rules of the Fleet, including indebted and crooked clergymen. Marriage houses were established in taverns and coffee-houses. Some ministers even conducted marriages in their own homes. A similar situation existed in the Mint, the area around the King's Bench Prison in Southwark.

The Fleet became the most popular centre for clandestine marriage in England. John Southerden Burn, in his 1846 *History of Fleet Marriages*, gives short biographies on eighty-nine Fleet parsons. Some went as far as to produce handbills promoting the services they offered, such as that by Revd Peter Sympson:

Insolvent Debtors – Common Law and Central Prisons and Records

'The Last Remains of the Fleet Prison'. Published in Old and New London, *Vol.2 (Cassell, Petter and Galpin, 1878).*

G. R.
At the true Chapel
At the old red Hand and Mitre, three doors from Fleet Street Lane
And next Door to the White Swan;
Marriages are performed by authority by the Reverend Mr. Sympson educated at the University of Cambridge, and late Chaplain to the Earl of Rothes
N. B. Without Imposition.

> From 25 March 1754, all clandestine marriages were made illegal by Lord Hardwicke's Marriage Act.
>
> The surviving registers of these clandestine marriages, held at The National Archives in Series RG 7, include an estimated 250,000 weddings between 1679 and 1754. These have all been digitized and are available on Ancestry and TheGenealogist.

The Fleet continued as a debtor's prison until 1842, when the Queen's Prison Act consolidated the Fleet, Marshalsea and Queen's Bench prisons into one, under the name of Queen's Prison. The Fleet was closed on 10 November 1842 and was sold to the Corporation of London for £25,000. The site was finally demolished in 1846.

MARSHALSEA PRISON

The prison was originally a branch of the Court of the Verge and Marshal, the disciplinary department of the medieval royal household (not to be confused with the Marshal of the King's Bench, who had responsibility for prisoners in the King's Bench Prison). In later periods it was a major debtors' prison, for persons committed for debt or contempt, by the Palace Court.

The Marshalsea was the smallest of the four main London debtors' prisons and housed both debtors and Admiralty prisoners: smugglers, those charged with excise offences, and sailors who had been court-martialled. Pirates were also held there. In the early-eighteenth century concern was shown by a committee of MPs that their presence would lead to other prisoners going further astray.

Originally, the Marshalsea Prison stood at Mermaid Court. In 1776, John Howard had described it as 'an old irregular building, or rather several buildings in a spacious yard'. By 1811 it was in an extremely poor state and its prisoners were moved to a new prison further down Borough High Street at Angel Court.

By the late eighteenth century the prison of the Marshalsea lay on a site adjoining the King's Bench Prison in Borough High Street, Southwark.

Insolvent Debtors – Common Law and Central Prisons and Records

'North View of the Marshalsea, Southwark before the New Buildings'. Published in Gentleman's Magazine, *May 1804.*

Writing in *All the Year Round*, Charles Dickens described the Marshalsea in 1728 as 'squeezing the prisoners for money "like apples in a cider press"'. There were fees for turning keys or for removing irons.

In 1776, John Howard's report of the Marshalsea stated:

Five [rooms] are let to a man who is not a prisoner: in one of them he keeps a chandler's shop; in two he lives with his family; the other two he lets to prisoners.

… The tap is let to a prisoner in the Rules of the King's Bench Prison; this Prison being just within those Rules. I was credibly informed, that on one Sunday in the summer of 1775, about 600 pots of beer were brought in from the public house in the neighbourhood (Ashmore's) the Prisoners not liking the Tapsters beer.

'Racquet Court of the Marshalsea Prison'. Published in Old and New London *Vol.6 (Cassell, Petter & Gilpin, 1878).*

In 1824 Charles Dickens's father was imprisoned in the Marshalsea, and in 1857 the prison was used as the setting for *Little Dorrit*.

When he finished *Little Dorrit* Dickens went on a nostalgic trip to the Marshalsea. He describes the scene in the preface:

> Wandering, however, down a certain adjacent Angel Court, leading to Bermondsey, I came to Marshalsea Place, the houses in which I recognised, not only as the great block of the former prison but as preserving the rooms that arose in my mind's eye when I became Little Dorrit's biographer. ... Whosoever goes into Marshalsea Place, turning out of Angel

Court, leading to Bermondsey, will find his feet on the very paving-stones of the extinct Marshalsea Gaol; will see its narrow yard to the right and to the left, very little altered if at all, except that the walls were lowered when the place got free; will look upon the rooms in which the debtors lived; will stand among the crowded ghosts of many miserable years.

As with the Fleet, the Marshalsea was abolished under the Queen's Prison Act 1842, and its prisoners were transferred to the Queen's Prison.

KING'S (QUEEN'S) BENCH PRISON AND QUEEN'S PRISON

By the eighteenth century, the King's Bench Prison had long been one of London's largest prisons for debtors. Originally located in Borough High Street, south of the River Thames, it was relocated in the 1750s to a new site, also in Southwark, ostensibly to provide fresh air for the prisoners.

The majority of the prisoners in the King's Bench Prison, from the fifteenth century on, were persons committed, on a plaintiff's writ of *capias ad satisfaciendum*, for undischarged liabilities following a civil action for debt or similar, a procedure abolished for most purposes by the Debtors Act 1869. Other, more short-term, prisoners were on remand pending trial, either under King's Bench local jurisdiction, or on transfer of their cases from inferior courts.

James Grant described the Queen's Bench Prison at length in his *Sketches in London*. The section commences:

> The Queen's Bench Prison ... is situated in the Borough of Southwark, and embraces, with its open space, about four acres of ground. The principal building is 300 feet in length, and has a good deal of the appearance of a barracks. The whole is enclosed by a wall 35 feet in height; and which, to render the assurance of the safe keeping of the inmates doubly

'King's Bench Prison, Principal Entrance'. Published in London and its Environs in the Nineteenth Century *(Jones & Co., London, 1829).*

sure, is surmounted by large iron spikes. The exterior of the building is gloomy, owing partly to the dingy hue of the bricks, and partly to the smallness and plainness of the windows. The entire number of rooms within the walls of the Queen's Bench Prison, is 225, of which eight are called 'state rooms', and are set apart for the better class of prisoners. Half-a-crown a-week is paid as rent for one of these rooms. For the other rooms, with the exception of a few back ones which poor prisoners occupy rent free, the inmates pay one shilling weekly, and have to provide their own furniture. If, however, two persons are appointed to the same room, they are only charged sixpence each; if three, only fourpence each. In addition to the

225 rooms, there are a coffeehouse and public kitchen, and a public-house. At one end of the prison there is a kind of market, consisting of several sheds, occupied by butchers, poulterers, green-grocers, &c., each tenant paying a weekly rent of one shilling. These shillings, with the amount received for the various rooms, go into the pockets of the Marshal, and are one source whence he receives his remuneration. His other sources are fees on commitments and discharges, or for granting the rules, or the liberty of living within the walls of the prison.

[…]

There are always, in addition to the butchers, green-grocers, &c., formerly mentioned, a number of tradesmen, prisoners in the Queen's Bench, who pursue their respective

'Interior of the King's Bench Prison'. Drawn by J.C. Whichelo and engraved by T.L. Busby. Published by G. Smeeton, 1812.

callings there. When I last visited the place, which was two months ago, I found almost all the apartments on the ground-floor tenanted by what Robert Owen would call the sons of industry. One of these rooms is converted into a sort of bazaar in miniature, brimful — that is to say, if one may judge from a passing glance at the window — of the most miscellaneous assortment of merchandise ever collected together; while no individual article could possibly have cost more than three-halfpence. Next door to this depot of small-wares, was a barber's shop.

It is claimed that squash was invented in the King's Bench Prison.

The King's Bench had a Marshal, Deputy Marshal, three or four turnkeys, a clerk of the papers and some tipstaffs who took people to court and back. Neither the King's Bench nor Fleet Prisons had any medical staff and inmates in both relied on the services of any doctors or surgeons who had the misfortune to be imprisoned with them.

The Marshal of the King's Bench made his living by renting out rooms and from admittance and discharge fees. The downside was that he could be sued if he allowed a debtor to escape, which happened fairly frequently during the eighteenth century. As well as fees, the Marshal of the King's Bench took a share of the profits from the 'Tap': the prison beer-house, sale of beer, along with rent for the coffee house and bakery. In 1815 the Marshal was making a profit of £3,500 a year from the prison.

By the Prison Act 1842 the Queen's (King's) Bench Prison was renamed the 'Queen's Prison'. It was appointed the only prison for debtors, bankrupts, and other persons who might previously have been lawfully imprisoned in any one of the three prisons. It also became the prison serving the Palace Court in succession to the Marshalsea Prison. The Queen's Prison was itself abolished by the Queen's Prison Discontinuance Act 1862, and the prison building was used thereafter as a military prison.

Insolvent Debtors – Common Law and Central Prisons and Records

WHITECROSS STREET PRISON

Whitecross Street Prison was built between 1813 and 1815 by the City of London in Whitecross Street as a debtors' prison for the exclusive reception of persons in the custody of the sheriffs on civil process for London and Middlesex who would otherwise have gone to Newgate, the two compters or Ludgate. The prison was capable of holding up to 500 prisoners, although in normal circumstances less than half that number would be held there. The majority of those ordered for imprisonment by the Courts of Requests were sent to Whitecross Street. In 1870 all prisoners were transferred to the new Holloway Prison.

James Grant, in his 1838 book *Sketches in London*, wrote:

> And such is the facility of the debtor and creditor law in consigning human beings to prison, that a person has only to go and swear a debt of a shilling or sixpence against any other party, before the City Court of Requests, to have that party, if unable or unwilling to pay the debt, shut up in this prison for twenty days. The number of persons annually committed to Whitecross Street prison is supposed to be very nearly 2,000. [The prison] is divided into three departments; the first is set apart for those persons who are freemen of the city of London, and is called the Ludgate side of the prison; the second is set apart for persons within the jurisdiction of the city, and is called the London side; and the third is appropriated to the reception of those arrested in the county, and is called the Middlesex side.

In *Mysteries of London*, a lengthy 'penny dreadful' series which began to be published by George W.M. Reynolds in 1844, the central character is committed to Whitecross Street Prison.

> 'What is your name?'
> 'Arthur Chichester.'

'Have you got your bread?'

'Yes.'

'Well – put it in that pigeon-hole. Do you choose to have sheets to-night on your bed?'

'Certainly.'

'Then that will be a shilling the first night, and sixpence every night after, as long as you remain here. You can, moreover, sleep in the inner room, and sit up till twelve o'clock. Those who can't afford to pay for sheets sleep in a room by themselves, and go to bed at a quarter to ten. You see we know how to separate the gentlemen from the riff-raff.'

'And how long shall I be allowed to stay up in the Receiving Ward?'

'That depends. Do you mean to live at my table? I charge sixpence for tea, the same for breakfast, a shilling for dinner, and four-pence for supper.'

'Well – I shall be most happy to live at your table.'

'How many prisoners, upon an average, pass through the Receiving Ward in the course of one year?'

'About three thousand three hundred as near as I can guess. All the Debtors receive each so much bread and meat a-week. The prison costs the City close upon nine thousand pounds a year.'

'Nine thousand a-year, spent to lock men up, away from their families!' exclaimed Chichester. 'That sum would pay the debts of the greater portion of those who are unfortunate enough to be brought here.'

The system of imprisonment for debt is in itself impolitic, unwise, and cruel in the extreme: – it ruins the honest man, and destroys the little remnant of good feeling existing in the heart of the callous one. It establishes the absurd doctrine, that if a man *cannot* pay his debts while he is allowed the exercise of his talents, his labour, and his acquirements, he *can* when shut up in the narrow compass of a prison, where his talents,

Insolvent Debtors – Common Law and Central Prisons and Records

his labours, and his acquirements are useless. How eminently narrow-sighted are English legislators! They fear totally to abolish this absurd custom, because they dread that credit will suffer. Why – credit is altogether begotten in confidence, and never arises from the preconceived intention on the part of him who gives it, to avail himself of this law against him who receives it. Larceny and theft are punished by a limited imprisonment, with an allowance of food; but debtors, who commit no crime, may linger and languish – and *starve in gaol*.

The prisoners were held in six separate 'wards', including a separate 'female ward'. Known both as 'Burdon's Hotel' (after one of the governors) and the 'Cripplegate Coffeehouse', the prison seems to have had a worse reputation than the other London debtors' prisons of the time due to the fact that it had common wards rather than individual rooms.

In her will, Nell Gwynne (1650–1687), the long-time mistress of King Charles II, left the following instructions to her executors:

Plaque commemorating 'Nell Gwynne's bounty' on the site of Whitecross Street Prison.

4. That hee would give one hundred pounds for the use of the poore of the said St Martins and St James's Westminster to be given into the hands of the said Dr Tenison to be disposed at his discretion takeing any poore Debtors of the said parishes out of prison and for clothes this winter and other necessaryes as hee shall find fit.

12. That his Grace would please to lay out twenty pounds yearly for the releasing of poore Debtors out of prison every Christmas day.

The £20 payment, known as 'Nell Gwynne's bounty', is remembered today on a plaque on the site of Whitecross Street Prison.

HORSEMONGER LANE PRISON

The prison, in Southwark, was constructed between 1791 and 1799. It was once the largest prison in Surrey and remained the county's principal prison and place of execution up to its closure in 1878. It was a common gaol, housing both debtors and criminals, with a capacity of around 300 inmates. A large proportion of its inmates consisted of persons committed on process issued by the Courts of Requests.

By 1859 the gaol was no longer known as 'Horsemonger Lane' following the road's change of name to Union Road (today, Harper Road), being renamed Surrey County Gaol (its alternative name, the New Gaol, should not be confused with the New Prison, located north of the River Thames in Clerkenwell). The gaol was demolished in 1881.

Edward Wedlake Brayley in his 1850 *A topographical history of Surrey* described the Surrey County Gaol:

On the south side of Newington Causeway, is the Horsemonger-Lane Gaol, and Surrey Sessions House, which were erected in pursuance of an act of parliament passed in

Insolvent Debtors – Common Law and Central Prisons and Records

Surrey County Gaol, Horsemonger Lane, early nineteenth century.

1791 ... The gaol is a quadrangular building, three stories in height above the basement; the keeper's house being in the centre, and overlooking all the yards. Three sides are appropriated to the confinement of felons, and one side for debtors; the latter are arranged in classes, vis.— master debtors, common debtors, inferior debtors, and female debtors. On the felons' side there are ten wards, with rooms for the reception of three hundred and sixty-four persons; and, including debtors, nearly four hundred individuals have been imprisoned here at one time. A day-room, airing-yard, and sleeping-cells, arc attached to each ward; and the lobbies (each of which is six feet and a half in width) are well ventilated. Here, also, are two infirmaries for the different sexes, several baths, and a well-arranged chapel in which the felon prisoners and debtors are seated in their respective classes; and the males and females screened from the sight of each other.

NEWGATE PRISON
Between 28 September 1785 and 28 September 1786, there were approximately 266 debtors in Newgate gaol. The number dropped to 154 from 28 September 1786 to 28 September 1787.

Newgate was the county gaol for Middlesex as well as for the City of London. It was founded by King Henry II in 1188 and was originally part of the gatehouse at Newgate. As well as remanded and convicted prisoners, it also held debtors. In May 1776 John Howard recorded that 46 debtors were imprisoned in Newgate.

RECORDS
The records of the London debtors' prisons are held in two record offices: The National Archives (TNA) and London Metropolitan Archives (LMA). TNA holds the records of the prisons in the City of London and Southwark, where most debtors were confined: the Fleet, the Marshalsea, the King's (later Queen's) Bench and the Queen's prisons. Records for Whitecross Street Prison are held at TNA and LMA, and those for Horsemonger Lane at TNA and Surrey History Centre. Newgate Prison also held debtors, with the records at LMA. These are all covered in this chapter.

The records of the other, smaller London prisons and compters are mainly held at LMA, with a small number at TNA: Giltspur Street Compter, Poultry Compter, Southwark Compter, Wood Street Compter and Ludgate Prison These are discussed in Chapters 7 and 8.

For those imprisoned for debt outside London, records are mostly going to be held locally. These are discussed in Chapter 9.

Many records were lost in 1780, in the Gordon Riots, which saw the destruction of at least eight London prisons and houses of correction. These included the Fleet and the King's Bench Prisons. The surviving records of the King's Bench, Fleet and Marshalsea prisons were transferred to the Marshal of the Queen's Prison under section three of the Queen's Prison Act 1842. As a result, for some surviving records, the actual prison involved cannot be positively identified, with these being mainly in PRIS 10.

Insolvent Debtors – Common Law and Central Prisons and Records

Ancestry has details of over 700,000 criminals detained in the Marshalsea, King's Bench and Fleet Prisons, as well as some for which the prison cannot be identified. They are fully searchable by name and date. However, these are only a very small proportion of records that are available at TNA.

FLEET PRISON

PRIS 1 consists of Commitment Books, 1686–1842 (gaps). These detail the commitment to the Fleet Prison of debtors unable to stand bail for themselves, and therefore committed until the bail was paid. They were held in the Fleet at the expense of their creditors. Entries include the commitment number, the name of the person committed, the date, the justice ordering the committal, and the charge (debt, bankruptcy or a claim for trespass damages). The commitment number can be useful in identifying further records relating to the debtor in PRIS 2.

Commitment Books	1686–94, 1699–1700, 1709–13, 1725–Jul 1729, Mar 1733–Oct1748, May 1778–May 1842 (for 1719–22 see PRIS 4/1)	PRIS 1/1-50
Commitments Files	1758–1842	PRIS 2/1–160
Discharges	1775–1842	PRIS 3/1–43
Commitment Book (otherwise in PRIS 1)	Oct 1719–Feb 1722	PRIS 4/1
Condensed versions of Commitment Books	1769–92, 1810–40	PRIS 10/21–26
Entry Books for Discharges. Available on Ancestry	1734–43, 1779–1842	PRIS 10/49–57
Habeas Corpus Book	1730–58, 1780–1842	PRIS 10/88–110

Alphabetical list of prisoners surrendering in accordance with the Release of Prisoners by Rioters Act, 1780 and the Destruction of Prisons by Rioters Act, 1781	Jul–Oct 1780	PRIS 10/137A/1
Similar list as above of those who did not surrender	no dates	PRIS 10/137A/2
A list of those who surrendered into the actual custody of the Warden of the Fleet Prison in accordance with an advertisement in the *London Gazette* of [blank] May, 1781	no dates	PRIS 10/137A/3
Prison Register	1822–34	PRIS 10/149–150
Prisoners discharged under the Insolvent Debtors Act	1780–81	PRIS 10/155/3
Prisoners Committed and Discharged	1697–1702	PRIS 10/157
Day Rule Books (possibly relating to Fleet Prison)	1748–1843	PRIS 10/179-200
Day Rule Books (possibly relating to Fleet Prison)	1808–11, 1814–16, 1822–41	PRIS 10/201–223

There are often further details in the margins of the books, including the date of the discharge of bail and the sum concerned, the date of imprisonment if applicable, and sometimes the names of the lawyers involved, or the date of death of the prisoner if they had not survived long enough to attend court. Correspondence concerning individual cases is occasionally to be found loose between the pages of the books.

It is uncertain if any Commitment Books existed before 1685. There are a number of gaps in the series. The gap from 1695–98 can be filled partly by the Fleet Commitment and Discharge Book, PRIS

Insolvent Debtors – Common Law and Central Prisons and Records

10/157. There is no means of obtaining information on commitments between 1729–33 and 1748–69. A lost book would account for the gap between July 1729 and March 1733. The missing books from October 1748 and May 1778 were burnt during the Gordon Riots in 1780. Those for October 1719–February 1721 are in PRIS 4/1.

Pieces /1–4 are in Latin. Thereafter the records are in English, conforming to the Proceedings in Courts of Justice Act 1731. For Pieces /1A and /2 there is a typescript index in TNA's search rooms. Piece /1B is indexed by in IND 1/10788. Pieces 3–50 have internal indexes to prisoners' names.

Example: Fleet Prison Commitment Book, 1813

Fleet Prison Commitment Files, June 1812–September 1813.

In 1813, John Barwick was committed to the Fleet Prison for 'want of bail' awaiting the case brought against him by Harriet Reedman to be heard:

> 15,804. John Barwick, On the 17th July 1813 was Committed &c. for want of Bail By the Hon~ble Mr Justice Chambre upon a Writ of Hab: Corp directed to the Sheriff of Middlesex and

by the return it appears that on the 13th July 1813 John Barwick in the said Writ named was taken by the said Sheriff and under his Custody detained by virtue of a Bill of Middlesex ret~ble before the King at Westm~ on Saturday next after the Morrow of All Souls to

1   answer Harriet Reedman Extrix of William Reedman dece~d in a plea of Tres: and also to her Bill agst the said John for £500, Debt upon Demand, according &c to be exhibited, Oths £240, & upwards Warry.

Also detained by virtue of Ano~r Writ of Cap: ad Resp: ret~ble before the King's Justices at Westmr on the Morrow of All Souls

2   to answer Thomas Faulkner in a plea of Tres: and also that the said John may answer the said Thomas according &c in a certain Pleas of Tres: on the Case upon promises to his Damage of £15 & upwds Debt upon Demand, Oath £15. Minchin by Neale.
20th July 1813.
by Warte of Plts Attys

Condensed versions of the Prison Commitment Books, 1769–1792 and 1810–1840, can be found in PRIS 10/21–26, which fill the gap in the main series for the years 1769–78.

Commitments Files, 1758–1842, PRIS 2/1–160 are files of documents of commitment, render and surrender concerning the committal of debtors and bankrupts to the Fleet Prison. Each file (the later ones are in bundles) relates to an individual prisoner. The documents include the writ of *habeas corpus* from the justice of the bench to the sheriff who detained the debtor, the sheriff's confirmation of arrest, and details of the debtor's discharge of bail by admission to the prison. Case numbers appear on the papers in these bundles, which can be cross-referenced to the Commitment Books in PRIS 1.

Information on cases mentioned in PRIS 2/107, Fleet Prison

Insolvent Debtors – Common Law and Central Prisons and Records

Commitment Files for 1811 December 26– July 7 1812 (nos. 14,862–15,177) will also be found in PRIS 1/26–27.

PRIS 2/1–157, 1758–May 1842 are arranged by commitment number (1–32,083). PRIS 2/158, 1814–February 1842 are comprised of various numbers. PRIS 2/159, June–November 1793 includes miscellaneous records. PRIS 2/160, July 1770–January 1842 relates to habeas corpus etc.

Example: Fleet Prison Commitment File, 1812
A Commitment File from 1812 includes information about William Morgan, then confined in the Fleet Prison:

> George the Third by the Grace of God of the United Kingdom of Great Britain & Ireland King Defender of the Faith &c To the Warden of our Prison of the Fleet ~~~~~ Greeting We Command you that you have the Body of William Morgan detained on our Prison under your custody so it is sayd under Safe and Secure conduct together with the Day and Cause of his being taken and detained by whatsoever Name he may be charged in the same before Sir Archibald Macdonald Knight Chief Baron of our Court of Exchequer at Westminster at his Chambers in Serjeants Inn Chancery Lane immediately after the Receipt of this Writ to do and receive all such things which our said Chief Baron shall then and there consider of him in this behalf and that you have there this Writ Witness Sir Archibald Macdonald Knight at Westminster the twenty third January in the fifty second Year of our Reign

PRIS 10/137A relates to the recapture of prisoners who were released from the Fleet Prison by participants in the Gordon Riots.

Debtors were freed when the plaintiff's opportunity to render a case against the defendant had expired, when the debt was paid off (usually through charitable means) or if the prisoner was freed in accordance with one of the frequent Insolvent Debtors' Acts.

Discharges, PRIS 3/1–43, 1775–1842 includes warrants addressed to the Wardens and gaolers of the Fleet Prison for the release of debtors in their care. Warrants are bundled by date, and the prisoner's commitment number can be used to trace records in other series. The information in PRIS 3 is to some extent replicated in Entry Books for Discharges, 1734–1743, 1779–1842, PRIS 10/49–57, which have the advantage of being indexed internally and available on Ancestry as 'London, England, King's Bench and Fleet Prison Discharge Books and Prisoner Lists, 1734–1862'.

The missing register, 1744–78, is explained on the flyleaf of the register commencing in 1779, PRIS 10/51:

> NB. the last Discharge Book (which contain'd Entries of Discharges for about twenty years past) was burn'd by the Rioters on the 7 June 1780, when the Prison was also destroyed.

These records are also available on Ancestry.

Habeas Corpus Books, 1730–1758, 1780–1842, 1845–1861, PRIS 10/88–112 are transcripts of the writs sent to the prison keepers ordering them to deliver prisoners to be charged at various courts. The gap in the books, between 1759 and 1799, is probably owing to destruction during the Gordon Riots in 1780.

Example: Habeas Corpus Book, 1815

An example from the Habeas Corpus Books for 1815 concerns Richard Ironmonger Forward, who was ordered to be delivered to the King's Bench Court 'three weeks from the day of the Holy Trinity':

> In the Kings Bench
> Moss & Phelps
> Received of the Warden of the Fleet the Writ of Habeas Corpus to him directed to bring up the body of Richard Ironmonger

Froward to the Bar of the Court of Kings Bench on Wednesday next after three Weeks from the day of the Holy Trinity. Dated 13 June 1815
Cooper & Lowe
Plts Attornies

The Prison Registers, 1822–1834, PRIS 10/149–150 record the name and number of the prisoner, when and by whom he was committed, the amount of debt he owed, the date of discharge and other remarks.

There are Day Rule Books (which probably relate to the Fleet Prison), 1748–1843, PRIS 10/179–223, the function of which is unclear, but which list names of prisoners, some in receipt of regular monthly payments.

Lists of Prisoners discharged under the Insolvent Debtors' Act, 1780–1781 are in PRIS 10/155/3.

Marshalsea Prison

Day Books of Commitments and Discharges Available on Ancestry.	Jan 1811–Nov 1842	PRIS 11/1–14
Specimens of documents scheduled for destruction	1786–1861	PRIS 11/20
Indexes to unidentifiable books, possibly from the Marshalsea prison	no dates	PRIS 10/151–154

Relatively few records of the Marshalsea survive and these mainly comprise Commitment and Discharge Books.

Day Books of Commitments and Discharges cover the period January 1811–November 1842, PRIS 11/1–14. (Although PRIS 11/14 is labelled as a 'Palace Court custody day book', the volume is a continuation of this series up to the closure of the prison in November 1842.) PRIS 11/1–14 is available on Ancestry as 'London, England, Marshalsea Prison Commitment and Discharge Books, 1811–1842'.

The Day Commitment Books record the name of the debtor brought into custody, the names of the creditor and attorney, and the damages and sums concerned. The books also record the discharges of the day.

Example: Marshalsea Prison Commitment and Discharge Registers, 1824

Marshalsea Prison Commitment Register: entry includes John Dickens (Dickins) on 20 February.

On 20 February 1814, John Dickens, father of Charles, was released from the Marshalsea prison, together with several other prisoners:

\multicolumn{6}{l}{A List of Prisoners brought into Custody and discharged on Friday 20 Feb. 1814}
Attorney	Names	At whose Suit	Damages	Sums Sworn
R	John Dickins	James Karr	40	10 & upwards
W	George Giles	Robert Ballenger	50	18 0 0
Arden	Francis Turner	William Browne	100	37 & upwards
Angell	William Cockburn	Thomas Spratley	---	26 & upwards

Specimens of documents listed for destruction, under schedule governing the disposal of public records of 26 October 1906, 1786–1861, PRIS 11/20 include original orders for discharges and subsidiary documents, from 1812 to 1842.

Indexes to books, possibly from the Marshalsea prison, no dates, are in PRIS 10/151–154. These include lists of names of prisoners, with page references to whichever book they once related.

King's (Queen's) Bench Prison and the Queen's Prison

Commitment Books	May 1747–Aug 1862	PRIS 4/2–54
Abstract Books of Commitments	Jul 1780–Oct 1815	PRIS 5/1–20
Discharges	1776–83, 1785, 1787–1862	PRIS 7/1–79
Execution Books	Michaelmas 1758–1852	PRIS 8/1–10
Rough version of Commitment Book	1850–62	PRIS 10/18–20
Day Books	1843–62	PRIS 10/38–41
Discharge Book	1857–62	PRIS 10/58
Habeas Corpus book	1843–61	PRIS 10/111-112
Prisoners that had surrendered in accordance with the Release of Prisoners by Rioters Act, 1780	Jul–Sep 1780	PRIS 10/136
Chronological list of prisoners who surrendered under the foregoing	Oct–Nov 1781	PRIS 10/137B/[1]
Alphabetical lists of prisoners for debt who are in the custody of the Marshal

Available on Ancestry | 1794, 1797, 1801, 1804, 1806, 1808, 1811–13 | PRIS 10/140–148 |
| Gaolers' Returns: Queens Prison (and Whitecross Street Prison) | 1862 | B 2/15 |
| Coroners' Inquests | 1746–50, 1771–1839 | KB 14 |

Commitment Books: May 1747–August 1862, PRIS 4/2–54 record the commitment of debtors to the King's (Queen's) Bench Prison, and its successor the Queen's Prison. Each entry is headed with the name of the debtor and the date on which he or she was admitted to the prison. Marginalia record the date of discharge or death in prison, and the sums involved. Many of the books contain indexes of inmates' names. The prisoner's discharge date or commitment number can be used to trace records in other series.

Rough versions of Commitment Books, 1850–1862, are in PRIS 10/18–20.

Example: King's Bench Commitment Book, 1813

Nicholas Boscawen was committed to the King's Bench prison in January 1813 for 'want of bail' and was to appear in court 'Saturday next after 8 days of Festival of St Hilary':

> 1539   Nicholas Boscawen Committed &c. 20th Jany 1813 for want of Bail upon a writ of Hab. Corps directed to the Sheriff of Middx and by the return it appears that on the 13 Jany 1813 he was taken and under the sd Sheriffs Custody detained by virtue of a writ of capias ad satisfaciendum re~ble before the King at Westmr on Saturday next after 8 days of Saint Hilary to satisfy Daniel Massey £80 debt and 80/- Levy £41-4-6 – Saunders
> Dis 23rd Feby 1818 per Plts Atty
> [...]

Abstract Books of Commitments, July 1780–October 1815, PRIS 5/1–20 are summaries of the details found in the later King's (Queen's) Bench Prison Commitment Books (PRIS 4). They are smaller, more portable versions, for easy reference. Some of the books duplicate the contents of the main books exactly, others are inferior copies containing only a number of the details in the originals. However, they have the advantage of being indexed and

Insolvent Debtors – Common Law and Central Prisons and Records

contain details of the date of commitment, the debt involved, the name of the prisoner, the prosecutor's name and the date of discharge. The information recorded here can be cross-referenced to the Warrants of Discharge in PRIS 7. The prisoner's discharge date or commitment number can be used to trace records in other series.

Warrants for Discharge of Debtors from the King's (Queen's) Bench prison, and its successor, the Queen's Prison, 1776–83, 1785, 1787–1862, PRIS 7/1-79 are filed by date of discharge and give the name of the prisoner, the date of his or her release, and the names of the other parties involved in the case. The prisoner's commitment number can be used to trace records in other series.

PRIS 10/58 comprises three small notebooks which were the Keeper's own condensed versions of the Discharge Books (PRIS 7) for the years 1857 to 1862. In them he recorded the date of the prisoner's commitment, the class of prisoner, and the date of discharge.

Example: King's Bench Prison Discharge Book, 1816

A Discharge Book for 1816 records Richard Bulloss being released from the King's Bench Prison under the 1813 Act for the Relief of Insolvent Debtors.

> 7503
> At the Court for Relief of Insolvent Debtors, holden at the Guildhall of the City of Westminster, on Wednesday the 27 day of March in the 56th Year of the Reign of His present Majesty, and
> In the Year of our Lord 1816, before Charles Runnington, Serjeant at Law,
> His Majesty's Commissioner for the Relief of Insolvent Debtors.
> In the matter of the Petition of Richard Bulloss committed as Richard Bolloss
> A prisoner confined in the Kings Bench Prison

Seeking the Benefit of the Act of the 53d Year of His Majesty's Reign, intituled "An Act for the Relief of Insolvent Debtors in England."

WHEREAS, upon the hearing of the matter of the Petition of the said Prisoner, this Court did amongst other things order and adjudge the said Prisoner to be entitled to the Benefit of the said Act: And whereas it appears to this Court, that the said Prisoner hath in all things conformed to the directions of this Court and the said Act of Parliament: This Court doth order the said Prisoner to be forthwith discharged from Custody as to Thomas Williams at whose Suit he is detained in your Custody

	By the Court
To the Marshall of the)	Thomas Hack
Kings Bench Prison)	Clerk

Execution Books, Michaelmas 1758–1852, PRIS 8/1–10 detail the execution of the debts and damages awarded of prisoners at the King's (Queen's) Bench Prison and the Queen's Prison. The entries include the names of the debtor, creditor and attorney, and the amount of the debt or damages with a record of the repayment. The date of discharge of the prisoner is given in the margin. The prisoner's discharge date or commitment number can be used to trace records in other series. Entries are arranged in alphabetical order of prisoners' names, and then under the term in which the debtors were admitted to the prison: Hilary, Easter, Trinity or Michaelmas.

Alphabetical lists of prisoners for debt who were in the custody of the Marshal, King's Bench Prison, 1794, 1797, 1801, 1804, 1806, 1808, 1811–13 are in PRIS 10/140–148. These are available on Ancestry.

Gaolers' Returns, for both the Queen's Prison and Whitecross Street Prison, May–September 1862 are in B 2/15.

Not all debtors were discharged from the King's Bench Prison

Insolvent Debtors – Common Law and Central Prisons and Records

before death struck. Coroners' inquisitions on dead prisoners from this prison, for the years 1746–50 and 1771–1839, can be found in KB 14.

Example: Fleet Prison Coroners' Inquest for Charles Ingram, 28 March 1800

In 1800, at a coroner's inquest, the jury found that Charles Ingram had 'accidentally thrown himself and fall from and out of a two pair of stairs Window'. More usually, the cause of death of prisoners was recorded as 'natural causes'.

> King's Bench Prison
> Southwark in the County
> of Surrey
> An Inquisition Indented taken for our Sovereign Lord the King at the Borough of Southwark in the County of Surrey in the King's Bench Prison there upon the Twenty eighth day of March in the Fortieth year of the Reign of our Sovereign Lord George the third by the Grace of God of Great Britain France and Ireland King Defender of the Faith &c before me James Templer Esquire Coroner and Attorney of our said Lord the King in the Court of our said Lord the King before King himself Upon View of the Body of Charles Ingram Esquire Lake a Prisoner Within the walls of the King's Bench Prison then and there being dead upon the Oath of William Pryer Robert Hatch Thomas Adams George Simpson Thomas Cole Law Kemp George Street Lun
> Jagger and Isaac Loader
> Prisoners as well within the Walls of the said Prison as the Rules thereof good and lawful Men of the County aforesaid then and there being dead sworn and charged to enquire for our said Lord the King when and how and in what manner the said Charles Ingram came to his Death who upon their Oath say that the said Charles Ingram upon the twenty Eighth

day off March instant being in a violent state of Intoxication did accidentally throw himself & fall from and out of a two pair of stairs Window of the Prison aforesaid to & against the ground & pavement there underneath by reason & means whereof the said Charles Ingram upon the Day & Year aforesaid within the Walls of the Prison aforesaid by the accident aforesd did die & not otherwise or in any other manner to the knowledge of the Jurors aforesaid In Witness whereof as well the Coroner & Attorney of our said Lord the King as the said Jurors have hereunto set their hands & seals the day & Year & at the place first above mentioned.
[signed by Coroner and jurors]

Day Books, 1843–62, PRIS 10/38–41 record daily deliveries, discharges and final settlements of debts of prisoners, along with the names of the attorneys concerned.

Habeas Corpus Books, 1843–61 are in PRIS 10/111–112.

Acknowledgements by prisoners, who were at large because of the fire on 7 June 1780, that they had surrendered in accordance with the Release of Prisoners by Rioters Act, 1780, are recorded, July–September 1780, in PRIS 10/136. The acknowledgements are signed by the prisoners and dated from the places where they were lodgers at the time of technical surrender.

Chronological list of prisoners, October–November 1781, PRIS 10/137B/[1] who surrendered under the foregoing Act, or should have done so and who in accordance with a proclamation of 20 October 1781, were required to become actual prisoners.

Whitecross Street Prison
Records held at The National Archives relating to Whitecross Street Prison consist of Gaolers' Returns, 01 May 1962–31 Dec 1869, and Examination of Prisoners both, in Series B 2.

Insolvent Debtors – Common Law and Central Prisons and Records

Gaolers' Returns	01 May 1862–30 Sep 1862, Nov 1864, 01 Jan–31 Dec 1868, 01 Jul–31 Dec 1869	B 2/15*, 16, 18–20, 22, 23, 25, 28, 29, 31 * Includes Queen's Prison
Gaolers Returns: Examination of Prisoners	01 Jul–30 Nov 1869	B2 /32

Records held at LMA relating to Whitecross Street Prison:

Names of prisoners in custody of Sheriffs in Debtors' Prison	Sept 1817	CLA/034/01/008
Prisoners removed from Giltspur Street to Whitecross Street	1815–19	CLA/025/WS/01/048
Liberate Fees to Sheriffs Memorials from the Sheriffs requesting compensation for the loss of gaol fees from debtors, giving the names of debtors discharged from Whitecross Street Prison (and Newgate)	1816–29	MJ/SP/L/001–014

Names of prisoners in custody of sheriffs in Debtors' Prison, September 1817.

The Names of the prisoners in the Custody of the Sheriffs of London and also of the Sheriff of Middlesex in the Debtors Prison for London and Middlesex delivered by Indenture by George Bridges Esquire and Robert Kirby Esquire late Sheriffs of the City of London and County of Middlesex unto Francis Desanges Esquire and George Alderson Esquire present Sheriff of the said City and County this 28th day of September 1817

Middlesex Debtors

By Process from the Courts of Westminster By Process from the County Court
[followed by names of debtors]

London Debtors

Ludgate   Poultry   Giltspur Street
[followed by names of debtors]

Horsemonger Lane Prison

| Gaolers' Returns | 1865, 1866, 1 Jul 67–30 Jun 1869 | B2/ 17, 21, 24, 26, 27, 30 |

Records held at The National Archives relating to Horsemonger Lane prison consist of Gaolers' Returns, 1865–30 Jun 1869, in Series B 2.

Newgate Prison

Most of the records which survive for debtors held in Newgate Prison that give details of prisoners are calendars of prisoners tried at the City of London and Middlesex Sessions. There are no registers of debtors. London Metropolitan Archives holds the following records:

Insolvent Debtors – Common Law and Central Prisons and Records

List of debtors	1762	CLA/040/08/008
Petition by 33 poor debtors	1742/3	CLA/040/08/009
Liberate Fees to Sheriffs Memorials from the Sheriffs requesting compensation for the loss of gaol fees from debtors, giving the names of debtors discharged from Newgate (and Whitecross Street Prison)	1816–29	MJ/SP/LJ/001-014
List of Insolvent Debtors (and in Whitechapel Prison)	1774	MJ/SD/030/014
List of Insolvent Debtors (and in Whitechapel Prison)	1781	MJ/SD/034/002
List of Insolvent Debtors in Newgate Prison	Jan 1772, 1772	MJ/SD/027/01, 24
List of Insolvent Debtors in Newgate Prison	1778	MJ/SD/033/53
List of Insolvent Debtors in Newgate Prison	1794	MJ/SD/036/45
List of Insolvent Debtors in Newgate Prison	1804	MJ/SD/041/50
List of Insolvent Debtors in Newgate Prison	1805	MJ/SD/042/03
List of Insolvent Debtors in Newgate Prison	1809	MJ/SD/044/83
List of Insolvent Debtors in Newgate Prison to be taken to Hick's Hall	1755	MJ/SP/1774/09/003

OTHER PRISON RECORDS

Series PRIS 10 at TNA includes many miscellaneous books of uncertain provenance owing to inadequate marking when the records of the three earlier institutions (King's Bench, Fleet and Marshalsea prisons) were placed together in 1842.

Chummage registers. These were books which recorded the numbers of single-occupancy and multiple-occupancy cells in the prison at weekly intervals.	1820–28, 1848–61	PRIS 10/7–14
Prisoners' complaints	1844–57	PRIS 10/114/3, 5, 6, 7
Prisoners' complaints, Applications for rooms, Prisoners' petitions	no dates	PRIS 19/115
Permits to have attendants Permits to go out	1816–32 1820–21	PRIS 10/113
Prisoners and securities	1735–57, 1828-30	PRIS 10/134–135
Alphabetical list of prisoners, presumably those who surrendered, with the names of their prosecutors, dates of (?) commitment and of discharge or death. All entries cancelled	no dates	PRIS 10/137B/2
List of prisoners in execution at the time of the fire of 1780 and of those committed and charged in execution while the prison was being rebuilt and who did not surrender under the proclamation of 20 Oct. 1781, giving prisoners' and prosecutors' names, the date (?) of commitment and the reason for commitment	no dates	PRIS 10/137B/3
Lists of prisoners discharged under the Discharge of Insolvent Debtors Act 1794 There is no evidence concerning the identity of the prison	1813–35	PRIS 10/138–139
Indexes	no dates	PRIS 10/155/1
Index if prisoners	1777–1832	PRIS 10/155/2
Index to register	1828	PRIS 10/155/4
Index to discharge book	1837	PRIS 10/155/5
° List of prisoners pursuant to the Act ° Prisoners committed and discharged pursuant to the Act	1754–1813 1842–62	PRIS 10/156

Insolvent Debtors – Common Law and Central Prisons and Records

○ Index of prisoners ○ List of prisoners who surrendered with the names of their prosecutors ○ List of prisoners surrendering in accordance with the Insolvent Debtors Act Available on Ancestry	1777–1814 1777–81 1780–81	
Lists of prisoners committed and discharged: contains rough lists of names of prisoners and dates of commitment or discharge	1777–81	PRIS 10/158
Fugitive book	1748–50	PRIS 10/158
Lists of prisoners committed and discharged: contains rough lists of names of prisoners and dates of commitment or discharge	1781–84, 1806–12, 1818–29	PRIS 10/159–164
Prisoners and securities	1822–25	PRIS 10/165–166
Register of Insolvent Debtors	1835–42	PRIS 10/168
List of prisoner's addresses, alphabetical	no dates	PRIS 10/171

Census Returns

Prisons were covered by the decennial census returns and should therefore appear in those for 1841, 1851 and 1861, imprisonment for debt ending in 1869. The references for the London debtors' prisons are as follows:

	1841	1851	1861
Queen's Bench Prison	HO 107/1084/10 ff.14-19	HO 107/1564 ff.232-237	missing
Fleet Prison	HO 107/726/6 ff.1-7		
Marshalsea Prison	HO 107/1085/9 ff.39-42		

Whitecross Street Prison	HO 107/727/12 ff.1-11	HO 107/1525 ff.416–423	RG 9/214 ff.153–155 (incomplete, folios 160+ missing) Initials only.
Giltspur Street Prison	HO 107/728/7 ff.15–20	HO 107 1526 ff.364–371	
Newgate Gaol, Old Bailey	HO 107/728/7 ff.6-12	HO 107/1526 ff.372–379	RG 9/217 ff.99-103
Surrey County Gaol (Horsemonger Lane)	HO 107/1065/12 ff.8–12	HO 107/1566 ff.252–256 ('Prisoners for Debt' ff.253-254)	missing

Chapter 7

INSOLVENT DEBTORS – LONDON COURTS AND COURT RECORDS

When it comes to researching ancestors from London, be it in the City or the wider metropolis, more often than not you need to throw out the rule book and think afresh. And typical of the differences you might encounter is when it comes to the handling of debt, debtors and bankrupts.

Apart from the three common law courts with national coverage, the system of trial and conviction was different in London and the metropolis to the rest of the county – and unfortunately more complicated. For most of the country, beyond London and Middlesex, research into miscreant ancestors, including debtors and bankrupts, from the sixteenth century onwards, is usually focused on the jury courts of the Assize and Quarter Sessions. However, for London and Middlesex there developed more complicated arrangements for dealing with those who broke the law.

Essentially, there was no assize *per se* and felons and other miscreants were tried mainly, but not exclusively, at the several Sessions of the Peace for the City of London or for Middlesex. Distinctions between the jurisdictions of the various courts could be blurred, particularly as the same justices frequently presided over different types of Sessions.

Historically, the City of London had been granted considerable judicial privileges by the Crown. No citizen was required to plead outside the City and, as a consequence, the royal courts also sat occasionally in the City at Guildhall. However, these sittings were wholly independent of the civic authorities. Over time, the City of London developed its own courts where the Mayor and Aldermen could settle disputes about town property, goods and chattels, wills and debts.

The Court of Husting was the supreme court of the medieval and later City of London. It was the oldest court in the City and, at one time, was the only court for settling disputes between citizen and citizen. As judicial business increased in the thirteenth century, the court was increasingly hampered by the fact that it sat only weekly and the sittings were alternately for Pleas of Land and for Common Pleas. Cases relating to mercantile law, personal actions and debt were over time transferred to the Sheriffs' Court and the Mayor's Court.

From 1444, the Mayor and Aldermen served as Justices of the Peace responsible for criminal trials in the City. Petty Sessions were held before the Lord Mayor, originally at Guildhall but from the mid-eighteenth century in the Justice Room at the new Mansion House. In 1737 a second Justice Room was set up at Guildhall, where regular sittings were held before one of the other Aldermen.

Importantly, there were several other local courts where most cases of debt were handled, where debtors could be tried and possibly committed to prison. These included the Mayor's Court, the Sheriffs' Court and the Courts of Requests, as well as several others.

Surviving records of all the London courts are more-or-less exclusively held at London Metropolitan Archives (LMA).

CITY OF LONDON COURTS
In the City of London, by the fourteenth century the obligation to repay a loan or to make future payment for goods already supplied was recorded in a recognizance made before the City Chamberlain and one or two Aldermen or before the Sheriffs. Here the debtor acknowledged that a debt was payable to the creditor and that in case of non-payment the debt should be levied from his lands, rents and goods.

Insolvent Debtors – London Courts and Court Records

A large number of these recognizances are recorded between 1274 and 1312 in Letter Books held at LMA.

| Letter Books A and B | 1274–1312 | COL/AD/01/001-002 |

These have been published as *Calendars of Letter-Books A & B*, edited by R.R. Sharpe (1899–1900) and are available on British History Online. For example:

Monday before the Feast of St. Valentine [14 Feb.], 20 Edward I. [1291-2], came Stephen de Folesham and acknowledged himself bound to George de Acre, merchant of St. Macaire in Gascony, in the sum of £10; to be paid, one moiety at Hokeday and the other at the Feast of Pentecost.

(The eve of the Assumption B. M., anno 20, the said Stephen paid the said George the sum of £7 3s. 2d. of the above debt, as the said George testifies, and there remains of the debt the sum of 56s. 10d.)

There are also twelve rolls of statutory recognizances of debt from 1285 to 1393 made according to the Statute of Acton Burnel and the Statute of Merchants of 13 Edward I to be taken before the Mayor and a clerk appointed by the King.

| Statutory recognizances of debt | 1285–1393 | COL/RG/01/001-012 |

Mayor's Court

The Mayor's Court developed out of business overflowing from the Court of Husting as an adjunct to the court. The Mayor's Court's main authority was to enforce the customs of London, including mercantile actions. From the early thirteenth century, the Mayor sat as the judge of the Mayor's Court, assisted by the Sheriffs and Aldermen. By 1259, complaints arising over delays in obtaining judgements in debt cases at the Court of Husting led to these being transferred to the Mayor's Court or the Sheriffs' Court.

The Mayor's Court became the pre-eminent court in the City, whereas the Sheriffs' Court was confined to the recovery of small debts. There was no monetary limit on the actions which could be heard in the Mayor's Court. It was less expensive than recourse to the royal courts at Westminster and, because of the speed with which suits could be dealt with, in comparison to other courts of the time, its business increased rapidly.

The first court roll dates to 1298, although proceedings were probably taking place before this, from around 1280. Many of the records of the Mayor's Court have not survived, especially those for the eighteenth and nineteenth century, which were either destroyed in a fire at the Royal Exchange in 1838 or with the Registrar's permission in about 1941. It is likely that there was also serious loss during the Great Fire in 1666.

Records at LMA relating to the Mayor's Court:

Early Mayor's Court rolls	1298–1307 (gaps)	CLA/024/01/01/001-009
Plea and Memoranda rolls	1327–1484	CLA/024/01/02/001-012
Files of Original Bills	1327–1733 (few before 1550)	CLA/024/02/001-321
Minutes and Actions	1679–1723	CLA/024/03/01/001-042
Books of Precedent	1603–1740	CLA/024/03/03/001-008
Files of Actions	1666–1705	CLA/024/04/001-040
Interrogatories and Answers	1628, 1646–1710	CLA/024/05/001-016
Depositions	1640–1738, 1803–35	CLA/024/06/001-065
Bills of Complaints and Answers	1654–1721	CLA/024/07/001-091
Papers relating to cases undertaken by James Gibson, attorney of the Mayor's Court	1691 and 1705	CLA/024/10/001-535
Calendar or list of Mayor's Court Interrogatories	1628, 1641–1710	CLA/024/011/001

Insolvent Debtors – London Courts and Court Records

The Early Mayor's Court rolls (incomplete), 1298–1307, CLA/024/01/01/001-009 have been published as *Calendar of Early Mayor's Court Rolls of the City of London, 1298–1307* edited by A.H. Thomas (1924) and are available on British History Online.

Plea and Memoranda rolls, 1327–1484, CLA/024/01/02/001-012 record the activities of the court which soon came to specialize in suits for debt. They have been published as *Calendars of Plea and Memoranda Rolls of the City of London 1323–1484* (7 volumes) edited by A.H. Thomas and P.E. Jones, 1924–61. The first three volumes, 1323–1412, are available on British History Online.

From the reign of Edward III onwards, files of actions or cases were kept, giving the declarations of plaintiffs, with short notes of the proceedings, judgements and executions, including full inventories of goods and chattels on which executions were made. Files of Original Bills, 1327–1733, are in CLA/024/02/001-321, but very few rolls survive prior to the reign of Elizabeth I. They are numerous for the sixteenth and seventeenth century and are of particular interest owing to the full inventories of goods and chattels on which executions were made.

Most of the original bills dating from before 1560 have been calendared on index cards. There is also an index to persons (plaintiffs, defendants and garnishees) appearing in the original bills and a list of schedules of goods among the original bills, 1565–1723.

Other surviving records for the Mayor's Court are listed in the table above.

Sheriffs' Court

London had two Sheriffs who each held a court at his compter – either the Poultry or Wood Street compter – which served as a prison for debtors and other prisoners. The Sheriffs' Courts handled cases of small debts and personal actions arising within the City. In 1785 the Poultry and Wood Street compters were demolished and prisoners were moved to the new Giltspur Street Compter in about 1791, where separate courts held by the two Sheriffs continued to be known as the Poultry Compter and Wood Street Compter. These courts were later transferred to the Guildhall and united into the City of London Court in 1867, finally being amalgamated with the Mayor's Court in 1921 to form the Mayor's and City of London Court.

The survival of the records of the Sheriffs' Courts is poor, probably because the Sheriffs retained custody of the rolls of the court during their year of office when they left, as they could be personally accountable if the administration of justice was called into question.

Records at LMA relating to the Sheriff's Court:

Court rolls	1318–1849 (many gaps)	CLA/025/CT/01/001-105
Plaints, accounts, proceedings, rolls of daily entries and issues tried	1653–1867 (many gaps)	CLA/CT/02/001-029
Poultry Compter: Commitment books	1792–1796, 1800–15	CLA/030/01/018-022
Poultry Compter: Minutes of actions	1769–1830	CLA/025/PC/01/001-025
Poultry Compter: Rolls	1832–57	CLA/025/PC/02/001-008
Poultry Compter: index to minutes of actions and rolls	1798–1841	CLA/025/PC/03/001-009
Wood Street Compter: Minutes of actions	1760–1833	CLA/025/WS/01/001-051
Giltspur Street Compter: Rolls	1823–49	CLA/025/WS/02/001-003
Wood Street and Giltspur Street Compters: Index to minutes of actions and rolls	1760–1841	CLA/025/WS/03/001-035

In 1814, John Robard brought a case against William Leathwicke for non-payment for the supply of various goods valued at £20.

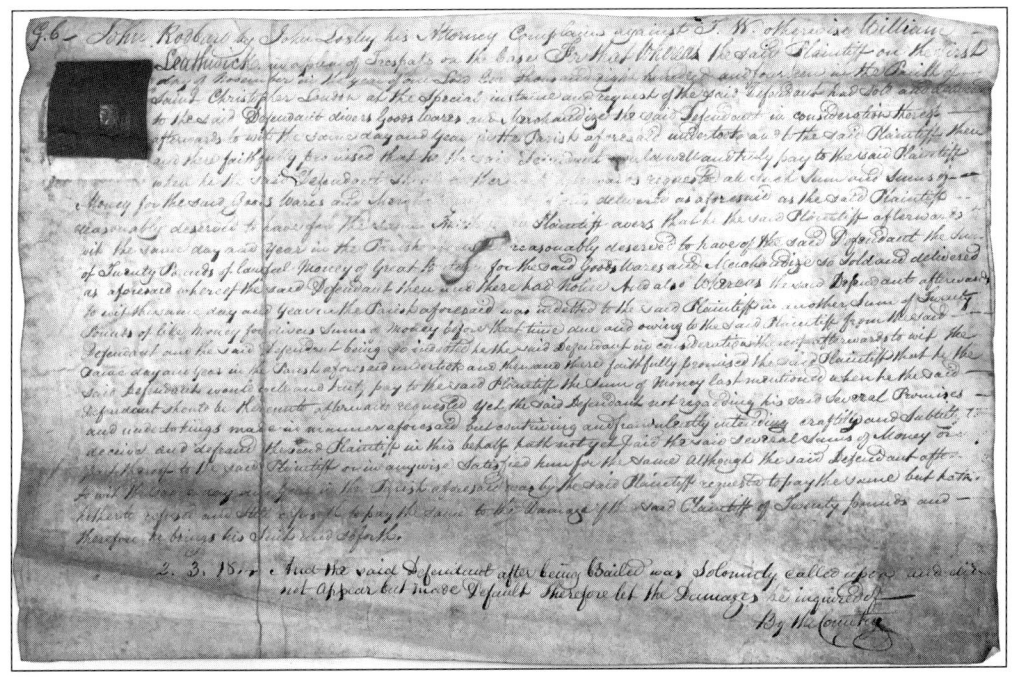

Insolvent Debtors – London Courts and Court Records

Sheriffs' Court Roll.

John Rodbard by John Losley his Attorney Complains against T. W. otherwise William Leathwicke in a plea of Trespass on the case For that whereas the said Plaintiff on the First day of November in the year of our Lord One Thousand eight hundred and fourteen in the Parish of Saint Christopher London at the special instance and request of the said Defendant had sold and delivered to the said Defendant divers Goods Wares and Merchandize the said Defendant in consideration thereof afterwards to wit the same day and year in the Parish aforesaid undertook and to the said Plaintiff then and there faithfully promised that he the said Defendant would well and truly pay the said Plaintiff when he the said Defendant (— unreadable —) requested all such sum and sums of Money for the said Goods Wares and Merchandize

(— unreadable —) and delivered as aforesaid as the said Plaintiff reasonably deserved to have for the same Merchandize Plaintiff avers that the said Plaintiff afterwards wit the same day and year in the Parish aforesaid reasonably deserved to have of the said Defendant the sum of Twenty Pounds of lawful Money of Great Britain for the said Goods wares and Merchandize so sold and delivered as aforesaid whereof the said Defendant then and there had notice And also whereas the said Defendant afterwards to wit the same day and year in the Parish aforesaid was indebted to the said Plaintiff in another sum of twenty Pounds of like Money for divers Sums of Money before that time due and owing to the said Plaintiff from the said Defendant and the said Defendant being so indebted he the said Defendant in consideration thereof afterwards to wit the same day and year in the Parish aforesaid undertook and theresaid there faithfully promised the said Plaintiff that he the said Defendant should be thereunto afterwards requested yet the said Defendant not regarding his said Several promises and undertakings made in manner aforesaid but contriving and fraudulently intending craftily and subtelly to deceive and defraud the said Plaintiff in this behalf hath not yet paid the sad several sums of Money or such part thereof to the said Plaintiff or in anywise satisfied him for the same Although the said Defendant after hitherto refused and still refuseth to pay the same to the Damage of the said Plaintiff of Twenty pounds and therefore he brings his Suit and so forth.

2.3.1814 And he said Defendant after being Bailed was Solemnly called upon and did Not appear but made Default Therefore let the Damages be inquired of

City of London Court

The City of London Court was formed when all Sheriffs' Courts were united in 1867. The court handled actions of debt and other personal actions arising within the City. The court was amalgamated with the Mayor's Court in 1921 to form the Mayor's and City of London Court, which still functions. Under the Courts Act, 1971 it was designated a County Court.

Records at LMA relating to the City of London Court:

| Suits and proceedings in equity | 1867–1919 | CLA/026/01/001-003 |

COURTS OF REQUESTS

Courts of Requests, sometimes referred to as Courts of Conscience, were established throughout the country, mainly during the eighteenth century. These were courts for the recovery of small debts by an easier, quicker, and cheaper process than existed in the other courts of law. By the 1830s there were sixty or so in total, with five in London and the metropolitan area. These were:

- Court of Requests for the City of London
- Court of Requests for the Borough of Southwark
- Court of Requests for Westminster
- Court of Requests for the Tower Hamlets
- Court of Requests for the County of Middlesex

The County Court Act of 1846 abolished all Courts of Requests.

The Southwark Court of Requests was established in 1749 for the borough of Southwark and surrounding parishes. In 1806, the jurisdiction was extended to include the eastern district of the Brixton Hundred. It could hear cases involving debts of up to five pounds and could imprison debtors for a maximum of 100 days. In 1830, 16,441 cases were tried at the Southwark Court.

The Westminster Court of Requests was constituted in 1750 and had jurisdiction over the parishes of St Margaret, St John the Evangelist, St Paul Covent Garden, St Clement Danes, St Mary-le-Strand, St George Hanover Square, St James and St Anne; and over that part of the Duchy of Lancaster which bordered the Liberty of

Interior of the Ancient Chapel of St Mary Magdalen, Guildhall: now the Court of Requests. Published by Robert Wilkinson, October 1817.

Westminster. Initially there were two courts, in Vine Street and Castle Street, but in the 1830s these were combined at Castle Street. The court could not adjudicate in cases involving debts above 40 shillings, and could not imprison debtors for more than seven days. In 1830, the number of cases tried was recorded as 15,439.

The Court of Requests for Tower Hamlets, established in 1750, was by far the busiest of the five courts. Initially it was restricted to adjudicate on debts under 40 shillings, but in the 1830s this was increased to five pounds. Within its jurisdiction were Whitechapel, Shoreditch, Norton Folgate, Bethnal Green, Mile End, Bow, Shadwell, Wapping, Ratcliff, Poplar and Stepney. In the late 1820s

Insolvent Debtors – London Courts and Court Records

the court was hearing nearly 30,000 cases each year, but the numbers dropped significantly thereafter.

The Middlesex County Court of Requests, also established in 1750, was situated in Kingsgate Street, Holborn. In the 1830s it was possibly hearing around 12,000 cases each year. When James Grant visited the Court of Requests for Middlesex in Kingsgate Street in the mid-1830s, he reported that:

> A more gloomy, ruinous miserable looking place inside is scarce to be entered. It is in striking keeping with the condition of the great majority of those who have business to transact in it.

No records appear to have survived for these last four Courts of Requests. However, for the Court of Requests for the City of London, there are series of records held at LMA, but only into the 1790s.

Court of Requests for the City of London

The jurisdiction of the court was confined to the City of London. This court was constituted by an Act of Common Council in 1518, under which commissioners were appointed to hear cases for the recovery of small debts not exceeding 40 shillings. Its jurisdiction was confirmed by Acts of Parliament, which by the late eighteenth century extended its jurisdiction to disputes under £10. In 1830, the number of cases decided was 9,502, but the use of the Court declined thereafter until it was abolished under the 1846 County Courts Act.

In 1838, James Grant wrote in *Sketches in London*:

> And such is the facility of the debtor and creditor law in consigning human beings to prison, that a person has only to go and swear a debt of a shilling or sixpence against another party, before the City Court of Requests, to have that party, if unable or unwilling to pay the debt, shut up in this prison for twenty days. The number of persons annually committed to Whitecross Street prison is supposed to be very nearly 2000.

Records at LMA relating to the Court of Requests:

Bonds and promissory notes	1613–1659 (many are unfit for production)	CLA/038/03/046-049
Index to names of debtors and creditors in above	1613–1659	CLA/038/01/011
Ledgers recording amounts to be paid into court in each suit, indexed	1698–1700, 1755-1786 (many gaps)	CLA/038/02/001-010
Court registers	1770–1790 (many gaps)	CLA/038/03/023-035
Alphabets or indexes to names of plaintiffs in court registers	1773–4, 1781–2, 1787–8	CLA/038/03/036-038
Summons books	1778–1796 (many gaps)	CLA/038/03/001-014
Warrant books	1776–1783, 1786–1794	CLA//038/03/016-019
Execution direction books	1789–1794	CLA/038//03/040-043

COUNTY COURTS

The County Courts as they now exist have their origins in the County Courts Act 1846, with modifications under the County Courts Acts of 1888 and 1934. The area of jurisdiction of each court is set from time to time by the Lord Chancellor. The original jurisdiction of the courts included claims of debt or for damages (except for libel, slander, seduction and breach of promise) not exceeding £400.

Records held by LMA, which date from before 1900, relating to the County Courts:

Bow County Court: Plaint and minute books	1847–1873, 1881–1882, 1892	CCT/AK/15/001-008
Edmonton County Court: Plaint and minute book	1894–1896	CCT/AK/46/001
Lambeth County Court: Summons minute books	1847–1848, 1854, 1864, 1874, 1884, 1894	CCT/AK/42/001-008

Insolvent Debtors – London Courts and Court Records

| West London (formerly Brompton) County Court: Minute, plaint and summons books | 1847–1899 (many gaps) | CCT/AK/43/001-013 |

SANCTUARY

There were areas of London apparently exempt from certain aspects of the law. Two statutes, one in 1377 and the other in 1379, recognized that Westminster, St Martin le Grand and other similar ecclesiastical liberties could offer refuge to debtors who honestly sought time to make repayment of outstanding debts, as against those who were frequently abusing the privileges. For several centuries, many debtors took 'sanctuary' in the precincts of various religious houses and other liberties, even after the Dissolution of religious houses in the sixteenth century. Unlike the ecclesiastical version of sanctuary, by which a fugitive could take temporary respite in a church, the secular version granted indefinite protection to debtors who wished to avoid arrest. Some debtors pre-empted the risk of being served with a writ by moving to a sanctuary as a means of encouraging their creditors to reach an agreement over repayment.

The most famous and notorious of these refuges was the former Whitefriars convent, nicknamed 'Alsatia', on the north bank of the Thames. A charter granted in 1608 by King James I, to the inhabitants of Whitefriars, appeared to acknowledge a certain measure of self-government and it soon became populated with the criminalized, especially debtors seeking refuge from bailiffs. It was not until 1697 that legislation and raids put an end to Alsatia. But even after that, there were still places in London that claimed to be outside the purview of the authorities.

The last surviving debtors' sanctuary was a district in Southwark known as the Mint, which stayed beyond the law until 1723. It was so named because a mint authorized by King Henry VIII was set up

'Alsatia' (Whitefriars). Based on Agas' map (published 1633).

in the area in about 1543. The mint ceased to operate in the reign of Mary I, but in the late seventeenth and early eighteenth century the area became known for offering protection against prosecution for debtors due to its legal status as a liberty.

Since debtors could not leave – except on Sunday, when no debts could be collected – it was unlikely they could work and so raise money to pay off their debts. Once there, debtors risked arrest if they were found outside of its boundary. Debt collectors, known as 'duns', waited on the roads out of the Mint for suspected debtors. Sometimes they were bill collectors in the modern sense, and sometimes thugs who beat and seized the debtor. Those who

Insolvent Debtors – London Courts and Court Records

attempted to leave on Sundays to get money from friends or lenders were called 'Sunday gentlemen', as they attempted to feign prosperity to deceive the creditors or their collectors.

Inside the Mint, life was hard. Debtors who went to the Mint frequently died of malnutrition or were murdered before raising enough money to pay off their creditors. The Mint was below the river's level and was consequently a breeding ground for both sewage and water-borne diseases.

Daniel Defoe describes life in the Mint for the heroine in his 1722 novel, *The Fortunes and Misfortunes of the Famous Moll Flanders*, which gives a rare view of the sanctuary through female eyes. It is due to her husband that Moll Flanders moves to the Mint; she is escaping his creditors rather than hers, and she takes the opportunity to change her identity and take on the role of widow.

> I went into the Mint too, took lodgings in a very private place, dressed up in the habit of a widow, and called myself Mrs Flanders.
>
> Here, however, I concealed myself, and though my new acquaintances knew nothing of me, yet I soon got a great deal of company about me; and whether it be that women are scarce among the sorts of people that generally are to be found there, or that some consolations in the miseries of the place are more requisite than on other occasions, I soon found an agreeable woman was exceedingly valuable among the sons of affliction there, and that those that wanted money to pay half a crown on the pound to their creditors, and that run in debt at the sign of the Bull for their dinners, would yet find money for a supper, if they liked the woman.
>
> However, I kept myself safe yet, though I began, like my Lord Rochester's mistress, that loved his company, but would not admit him farther, to have the scandal of a whore, without the joy; and upon this score, tired with the place, and indeed with the company too, I began to think of removing.

It was indeed a subject of strange reflection to me to see men who were overwhelmed in perplexed circumstances, who were reduced some degrees below being ruined, whose families were objects of their own terror and other people's charity, yet while a penny lasted, nay, even beyond it, endeavouring to drown themselves, labouring to forget former things, which now it was the proper time to remember, making more work for repentance, and sinning on, as a remedy for sin past.

But it is none of my talent to preach; these men were too wicked, even for me. There was something horrid and absurd in their way of sinning, for it was all a force even upon themselves; they did not only act against conscience, but against nature; they put a rape upon their temper to drown the reflections, which their circumstances continually gave them; and nothing was more easy than to see how sighs would interrupt their songs, and paleness and anguish sit upon their brows, in spite of the forced smiles they put on; nay, sometimes it would break out at their very mouths when they had parted with their money for a lewd treat or a wicked embrace. I have heard them, turning about, fetch a deep sigh, and cry, 'What a dog am I! Well, Betty, my dear, I'll drink thy health, though'; meaning the honest wife, that perhaps had not a half-crown for herself and three or four children. The next morning they are at their penitentials again; and perhaps the poor weeping wife comes over to him, either brings him some account of what his creditors are doing, and how she and the children are turned out of doors, or some other dreadful news; and this adds to his self-reproaches; but when he has thought and pored on it till he is almost mad, having no principles to support him, nothing within him or above him to comfort him, but finding it all darkness on every side, he flies to the same relief again, viz. to drink it away, debauch it away, and falling into company of men in just the same condition with himself, he repeats the crime, and thus he goes every day one step onward of his way to destruction.

Defoe himself had a chequered business career, which included bankruptcy, seizure of his property, imprisonment and possibly refuge in Southwark. He was a proponent of bankruptcy reform, playing a role in the passage of the 1705 Act to Prevent Frauds Frequently Committed by Bankrupts. He was, however, a firm critic of the sanctuaries, calling them 'those nurseries of rogues'.

In the same year as *Moll Flanders* was first published, the Mint lost its protected status as a result of the The Mint in Southwark Act:

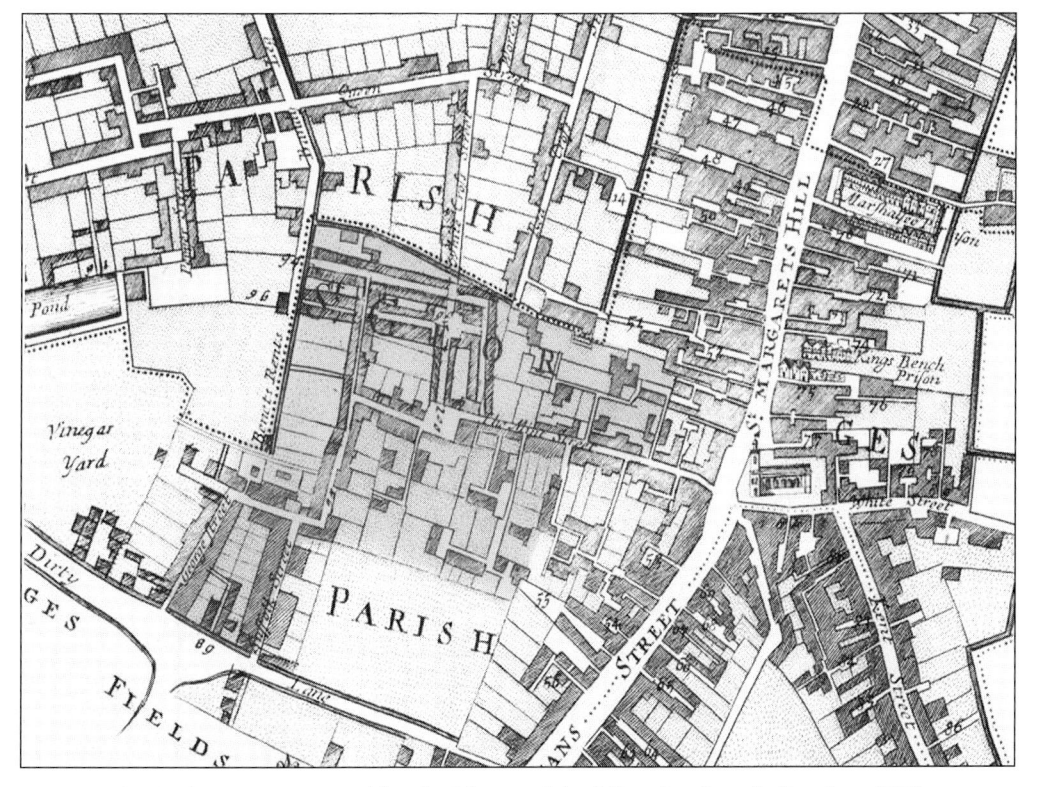

Approximate area covered by the Liberty of the Mint, Southwark. Based on 1720 map.

for more effectual execution of justice in a pretended privileged place in the parish of Saint George in the county of Surrey, commonly called the Mint; and for bringing to speedy and exemplary justice such offenders as are therein mentioned; and for giving relief to such persons as are proper objects of charity and compassion there.

At the same time, imprisonment for debts of less than £50 was abolished. The final clause of the Act offered an amnesty to those Minters, discharging debts below £50, albeit at the cost of 'assigning all their estates and effects whatsoever, for the benefit of their creditors'. Some 6,254 people applied for this relief, their names, trade or status and parishes being published over ten months, from February 1723, in the *London Gazette*.
London Gazette, 11 June 1723, Issue 6172:

… Having taken Shelter or Protection in a certain Place called Suffolk-Place, or the Mint, in the Parish of St. George Southwark, in the County of Surrey, on or before the 11th Day of February, 1722, and having petitioned one of His Majesty's Justices of the Peace for the said County, and his Warrant signed thereupon (together with a Writing, importing Notice thereof to all Creditors of the aforesaid Persons) directing them to appear at the next General Quarter-Sessions of the Peace to be held for the said County at Guilford, on Tuesday the 16th of July next, to be discharged, pursuant to an Act lately passed for giving relief to such Persons as are proper Objects of Charity and Compassion there, &c. and they conforming themselves in all things as the Act directs, their respective Creditors are to take Notice thereof.

The Society of Genealogists in London, holds the typescript *Petitioners against imprisonment for debt listed in the 'London Gazette', 1712-24; debtors in London with list of prisons, 1712-20; debtors taking sanctuary in the Mint in Southwark & petitioners list*, compiled by Ralph Hall (1990). The last section is a transcript of the entries in the *London Gazette* of those debtors who applied for relief under the 1722 Act.

Following the closure of the Southwark Mint in 1722, some refugees crossed the Thames and set themselves up in the Wapping, or New Mint. This survived for just over two years, being closed down by a further Act in 1724.

> Weaver. Ralph Williamson late of Newgate-street, Watchmaker. Thomas Hodgson late of Capenwrea-Hall in the Parish of Bolton by the Sands in Lancashire, Husbandman. John Read late of St. Saviour's Southwark in Surry, Horse-Chapman. Samuel Prince late of Oakingham in Berkshire, Mercer. John Winnard late of Clerkenwell in Middlesex, Gent. John Crosby late of Poplar in Stepney Middlesex, Shipwright. William Davis late of East-Smithfield in the Parish of St Bartholomew Aldgate in Middlesex, Barber-Surgeon. John Bland late of Leicester-Fields in Middlesex, Gent. Jacob Mestivier late of St Martin's in the Fields, Distiller. Henry Hicks late of Yaxley in Huntingtonshire, Woollcomber. Peter Pineda late of Grafton-street, Westminster, Silversmith. John Wyatt late of Greenwich in Kent, Surgeon. John Davis late of St. Saviour's Southwark, Weaver. Richard Haslip late of Gutter-Lane, London, Perfumer. Sebastian Hebden, Victualler, and William Harvey, Blacksmith, both late of St Giles's in the Fields. Henry Alloway late of St Bridget's, alias St. Brides, Seedsman. Richard Bennett, late of St James's Clerkenwell, Brewer. Having taken Shelter or Protection in a certain Place called Suffolk-Place, or the Mint, in the Parish of St. George Southwark, in the County of Surrey, on or before the 11th Day of February, 1722. and having petitioned one of His Majesty's Justices of the Peace for the said County, and his Warrant signed thereupon (together with a Writing, importing Notice thereof to all the Creditors of the aforesaid Persons) directing them to appear at the next General Quarter-Sessions of the Peace to be held for the said County at Guilford, on Tuesday the 16th of July next, to be discharged, pursuant to an Act lately passed for giving Relief to such Persons as are proper Objects of Charity and Compassion there, &c. and they conforming themselves in all things as the Act directs, their respective Creditors are to take Notice thereof.

London Gazette, 11 June 1723, Issue 6172.

Chapter 8

INSOLVENT DEBTORS – LONDON PRISONS AND RECORDS

As described previously, the procedure for bringing miscreants to trial and the trial process itself was different in the metropolis to the rest of the country. Once tried and found guilty, there were numerous prisons to which the debtors could be committed.

LONDON'S COMPTERS
Compters – sometimes referred to as counters – were small prisons for minor offenders such as religious dissenters, drunks, prostitutes and the like. But overwhelmingly, the inmates were debtors. The earliest compters dated from medieval times, but they were all closed by the middle of the nineteenth century, their inmates having been distributed to other prisons.

London had two compters north of the river (Wood Street and Poultry) and one to the south (Borough). Both Wood Street and Poultry compters were succeeded by Giltspur Street Compter in 1791.

Poultry Compter
Poultry Compter was run by one of the Sheriffs of the City of London from medieval times until 1815. It took its name from its location on a section of Cheapside called Poultry, itself named after the produce that was once sold in street markets along the thoroughfare. It was said to be the only prison in London with a ward set apart for Jews

Insolvent Debtors – London Prisons and Records

The Poultry Compter (published in London Old & New, *Vol.1).*

(probably because of its vicinity to Old Jewry). It was the only prison in London that was not attacked during the Gordon Riots, possibly because of General Gordon's strong Jewish sympathies. The compter was also known for its black prisoners, who were almost all ex-slaves, and whose status was ambiguous under law. Poultry Compter held ninety debtors in 1776. The compter was demolished in 1817.

Records held at LMA relating to Poultry Compter:

Commitment books	1792–1796, 1800–1815	CLA/030/01/018-022
List of prisoners	1724	CLA/030/02/006
List of debtors	1764	CLA/040/08/008

EXAMPLE: A LIST OF DEBTORS IN THE POULTRY COMPTER, 1764

A List of Debtors in the Poultry Compter			
		£ s d	£ s d
William Miles – at the Suit of Edward Wallis – Debt 5£ & upwds	Compoundd for	3.3.0	
	Fees	16.8	3.19.8
Edmund Poor – at the Suit of John Bell – on Execution for		1.7.8	
	Fees	16.8	2.4.4
Sarah Duburch – at the Suit of George Rusted – Debt 2£ & upwds	Ditto for	2.0.0	
	Fees	16.8	2.16.8
Mary Morrice – at the Suit of William Morrice – Debt 10£ & upwds	Ditto for	1.16.0	1.16.0
[etcetera]			

Wood Street Compter

Wood Street Compter replaced a medieval compter in Bread Street in 1555. It was rebuilt in 1670. It held sixty-nine debtors in 1776. Prisoners were moved from Wood Street to Giltspur Street in 1791, part of which was known as Wood Street Compter. The old premises were demolished in January 1792.

Records held at LMA relating to Wood Street Compter:

Insolvent Debtors – London Prisons and Records

Lists of prisoners handed over by the Sheriffs to their successors on 28 September annually (Indexed).	1741–1791 (gaps)	CLA/028/01/001-027
List of prisoners for debt in Wood Street Compter on 5 May 1788 with subsequent committals to November 1803	1788–1803	CLA/028/01/041
Names of prisoners sent from Wood Street Compter to Ludgate and Newgate	1770–1829	CLA/028/02/001-003
List of debtors. Includes pleas for charity (H M Bounty)	1764	CLA/040/08/008
Petition from debtors	1780	CLA/040/08/009

EXAMPLE: LIST OF DEBTORS IN WOOD STREET COMPTER, 1764

	A list of the Poor Prisoners for Debt in Woodstreet Compter			
	Their Names	When Committed	Their Debt	Compounded for	Total
			£. s. d	£. s. d	£. s. d
2 Plaintiffs	William Sacon	26th October 1761	18.0.0	4.10 Fees 16.8	5.6.8
	William Green	22nd September 1767	18.0.6	3.15 Fees 16.8	4.11.8
3 Plaintiffs	Isaac St..oy	29th October 1763	9.	4.14.4 Fees 16.8	5.11.
	Alexander Roch	11th November 1763	11.	4.0.0 Fees 16.8	4.16.8

EXAMPLE: PETITION FOR CHARITY, WOOD STREET COMPTER, 1764

In 1764, John Hunt applied for charitable relief:

> Wood Street Compter
>
> Sir
>
> Pardon my freedom of this application finding my self not taken notice of in this Charity makes me trouble you with my Necessitous case I was arrested on two Actions on the 2 Instant one for three Pounds five shillings the other four pounds five shillings the first debt being Superseded I only remain for the Debt of four pounds five shillings which being Unable to pay must remain in this destressed Condition without your kind relief of this Charity therefore most Humbly implore you to make me an Object of this Charity which Benevolance shall be repaid by the Sinceir Prayers and thanksgiving of Sir your Obediant and most Humble Servant John Hunt
>
> 12 April 1764

Wood Street Compter: Petition for charity.

Wood Street Compter
Sir,
Pardon my freedom of the application finding my self not taken notice of in this Charity makes me trouble you with my Necessitous case I was arrested on two actions on 2d Instant one for three pounds five shillings the other four pounds five shillings the first debt being Supersedable I only remain for the Debt of four pounds five shillings which being unable to pay must remain in this destressed condition without your kind relief of this Charity therefore must humbly implore you to make me an Object of this Charity which Benevolance shall be repaid by the sinceir Prayers and thanksgiving of Sir your Obedient and must Humble Servant
John Hunt
12th April 1764

Giltspur Street Compter

An Act of Parliament in 1785 had empowered the City of London Corporation to pull down the Poultry and Wood Street compters and to build a new compter in Giltspur Street, designed by George Dance the Younger. Giltspur Street Compter opened in 1791, replacing Wood Street and absorbing some of Poultry's inmates when that institution closed in 1817. It was based in Smithfield, opposite Newgate Prison. There was a plan to convert the compter into a fully-fledged prison in 1819, but nothing came of it. Giltspur Street was eventually closed in 1853 and demolished two years later, in 1855.

Separate sections were known as the Poultry and Wood Street compters after the courts held by the two Sheriffs themselves known as the Poultry Compter and Wood Street Compter, reflecting their earlier origins.

Records held at LMA relating to Giltspur Street Compter:

Tracing Your Insolvent Ancestors

Prisoners' lists, indexed	1791–1815	CLA/028/01/027-040, CLA/033/01/007
Prisoners committed by order of Court of Requests	1811–1823	CLA/030/01/023
Debtors' warrants	1801–1815	CLA/040/08/001-002
Prisoners removed from Giltspur Street to Whitecross Street	1815–1819	CLA/025/WS/01/048

Prisoners committed by order of the Court of Requests, 1811–1823, from September 1815, gives name, age, brief physical description, trade, and place of birth; from 1811 to 1816 it includes lists of prisoners discharged.

Giltspur Street Compter, 1840 (published in London Old & New, *vol.2).*

EXAMPLE: PRISONERS COMMITTED BY ORDER OF COURT OF REQUESTS, 1814

An example from the series refers to Bartholomew Winkler, committed at the suit of James Ellis and Thomas Perry (LMA: CLA/030/01/023):

Insolvent Debtors – London Prisons and Records

The Names of the Prisoners committed by order Of the Commissioners of the Court of Requests in London To the Giltspur Street Compter. Dated Sept. 28. 1811

28 Discha 2.9. 1814 by pay^t of Debt & Coast for J. Hicks J. Shannon	Bartholomew Winkler June 1. 1814	Yates
	By Execution ats James Ellis & Thomas Perry (60 days)	£3.10.0

Southwark Compter

The City of London was granted jurisdiction over the Borough of Southwark by royal charters from 1327. A further charter in 1550 made the inhabitants subject to city law and extended the jurisdiction of the City courts.

Southwark Compter (also known as Borough Compter) was the only compter south of the river. The City initially used part of the former church of St Margaret Southwark as a courthouse and compter. It moved to Tooley Street in 1717. It was overwhelmingly a debtors' prison, but also held a small number of criminals over the years. The establishment of a regular magistracy in 1814 led to a large increase in the number of prisoners, including debtors. In 1840 the City decided to use the Southwark Compter for female prisoners and female inmates were transferred there from Giltspur Street Compter. Southwark Compter closed in 1852 and was demolished in 1855.

Records held at LMA relating to Southwark Compter:

Lists of prisoners	1814–1842	CLA/031/01/010-013
		CLA/031/03/004
Committals for debt	1811–1830	CLA/031/01/001-002
Weekly return of the names of prisoners distinguishing debtors, misdemeanours etc, prisoners committed to Sessions, prisoners upon orders with particulars, as appropriate of debt, offence, sentence etc	1815–1818	CLA/031/02/017

Example: Committals for debt, Southwark Compter, 1818

Southwark Compter: Committals for Debt.

Folio	when committed	Defendants	Parish	Plaintiffs	With Costs Debts levied £. s. d.	Debts Original £. s. d.
			January 1818			
119C	17th	Edward Peplow	Lambeth	John Jones	1. 0. 5	0. 13. 0
303B	17	William Stopping	St Sav[rs] Clink	John Wild	1. 9. 11	1. 1. 0
46C	17	William Piercey	Bermondsey	Samuel Watkins	1. 4. 11	1. 16. 0

Officers	January 1818	
	How Discharged	
Clark	Discharged by Order from the Office sign[d] Speck & Meymott 19th Jan[y]	J. law
Whittince	Discharged by Philan[c] Soc[y] Mile End paying 15/- and a Order from the Office 5th Feb[y]	J. Law
Hudson	Discharged by Order from the Office sign[d] Speck & Meymott 19th Jan[y]	J. Law

WHITECHAPEL PRISON

This prison held debtors sentenced by courts serving the manors of Stepney and Hackney. There was an attempt in 1707 by the constables and other officers of Tower Hamlets to have it used also for petty criminal offenders, to save them the trouble of carrying prisoners all the way to the Middlesex house of correction or New Prison in Clerkenwell, but this was rejected by the Middlesex Justices in 1708.

In the 1777 edition of *The State of the Prisons in England and Wales*, John Howard reported:

> In it are confined those whose debts are above £2, and under £5. The master's-side prisoners have four sizeable chambers, fronting the road; i.e. two on each story. They pay 2s. 6d. a week; and lie two in a bed; two beds in a room. The common-side debtors are in two long rooms in the court, near the tap room; men in one room, women in the other; the court-yard is common. they hang out a begging-box from a little closet in the front of the house; and attend it in turn. It brings them only a few pence a day; and this pittance none partake but those who at entrance have paid the keeper 2s. 6d. and treated the prisoners with half a gallon of beer. When I was there in 1777, no more than three had purchased this privilege.

Records at LMA relating to the Whitechapel Debtors' Prison:

Orders to be discharged	1778	MJ/SD/020
List of Insolvent Debtors (and in Newgate Gaol)	1774	MJ/SD/030/014
List of Insolvent Debtors	1776	MJ/SD/031/005
List of Insolvent Debtors (and in Newgate Gaol)	1781	MJ/SD/034/002
Poor prisoners requesting a hearing and discharge under the Act for the release of insolvent debtors	July 1696	MJ/SP/1696/07/018
List of insolvent debtors to be discharged	July 1778	MJ/SP/1778/07/119

LUDGATE PRISON

Ludgate Prison was established in 1378 in the gatehouse of the Ludgate. By the eighteenth century it had moved to the former bridewell of the London Workhouse in Bishopsgate Street. It was used to imprison debtors who were Freemen of the City of London and for clergymen, proctors and attorneys who were held for minor offences. Twenty-nine debtors were confined there in 1776. Prisoners were moved from Ludgate Prison to Giltspur Street Compter in 1795. It was closed soon after.

Records at LMA relating to Ludgate Prison:

Prisoners' lists	1725, 1760, 1800, 1807–1815	CLA/033/01/007, 009, 014
List of debtors	1762	CLA/040/08/008
Debtors' warrants	1804–1814	CLA/040/08/002
Lists of prisoners discharged	1808–1815	CLA/033/01/010

The Prisoners Lists, CLA/033/01/009 (January 1724/25) include papers relating to the removal of prisoners from Ludgate to the London Workhouse, proposed as a prison which 'should be the prison for debtors being freemen of the City of London'.

PRISONERS INQUESTS

LMA holds inquest records for the City's prisons (including Newgate, Bridewell, Ludgate and the compters) and the Fleet.

Prison Inquests	1783-1839 (gaps)	CLA/041/PI

RELEASE OF INSOLVENT DEBTORS IN THE CITY OF LONDON

City of London Sessions records, held at LMA, include records relating to prisoners for debt who were seeking to be discharged from prison in the City of London under various Acts of Parliament for the relief of insolvent debtors. In the mid-eighteenth century many debtors applied from places overseas for the benefit of the

Acts. From 1794 proceedings are entered in the series of Sessions Minute Books (Peace).

Insolvent Debtors sessions books	1691–1773	CLA/047/LJ/09/001-014
Sessions of the Peace minute books	1794–1819	CLA/047/LJ/06/002-007
Debtors' schedules (unspecified prisons)	1671–1745 (many gaps)	CLA/047/LJ/17/013-023
Debtors' schedules (named prisons and compters)	1748–1820	CLA/047/LJ/17/024-094
Debtors' schedules (named prisons and compters)	1753–1757	CLA/047/LJ/17/095-120

The papers give the name, place of residence and occupation of the debtor, with the name and addresses of any creditors (i.e. those who owe money to the debtor) and any other incidental information. There is a card index to debtors.

Example: Insolvent Debtors Sessions Book, 1765

Prisoner in the Gaol of Newgate for Debt
John Dunn in the Keepers List as a Prisoner on the 19th
   February 1765 upon process issuing out of The Court of
   Requests commonly called the Court of Conscience
   and in 3 Gazettes   Dd
Prisoners for Debt in the Poultry Compter
Mordecai Levy in Do as a Prisoner on the 26th February
   1765 upon Do and in Do   Dd
James Preedy in Do as a Prisoner on the 14th January
   1765 upon Do and in Do   Dd
George Young in Do as a Prisoner on the 29th April
   upon Do and in Do   Dd
Prisoners for Debt in Woodstreet Compter
George Middleton in Do as a Prisoner on the 22nd
   January 1765 upon Do and in Do   Dd

The Debtors' schedules cover prisoners applying from the Fleet Prison, Ludgate Prison, Newgate Prison, Wood Street Compter, Poultry Compter, Giltspur Street Compter and Borough (Southwark) Compter.

Example: Debtors Schedule, 1773.

London
To wit.)   To the Warden of the Fleet prison
)   or his Deputies
                  Whereas Timothy Gard formerly of the Paris
                  of St Paul Shadwell in the County of Middlesex
                  late of Brussels in Brabant Merchant has
                  petitioned me Frederick Bull Esqr Lord Mayor of
                  the City of London and ~~~~~ one of his
                  Majesty's ~~~~~ setting forth, that he was a
                  Fugitive for Debt, and beyond the Seas in
                  Foreign Parts on the First Day of January, 1772,
                  and being since returned, hath surrendered him
                  self a Prisoner unto you, within Fourteen Days
                  after his landing, and praying for the benefit of
Fredk Bull   an Act of Parliament made in the Twelfth Year of
Mayor   Parliament made in the Twelfth Year of his
                  present Majesty King George III, intitled, An Act
                  for the Relief of insolvent Debtors; these are to
                  authorize and require you to bring the Body of
                  the said Timothy Gard ~~~~~ before his
                  Majesty's Justices of the Peace, at the next
                  Session of the Peace, to be held at Guildhall
                  ~~~~~ In and for the said City of London on
                  the Sixth Day of December next, or any
                  Adjournment Thereof, to be held next after the
                  Expiration of Ten Days from the date hereof, at
                  Ten of the Clock in the Forenoon, in order to his
                  being released and discharged out of Custody,

Insolvent Debtors – London Prisons and Records

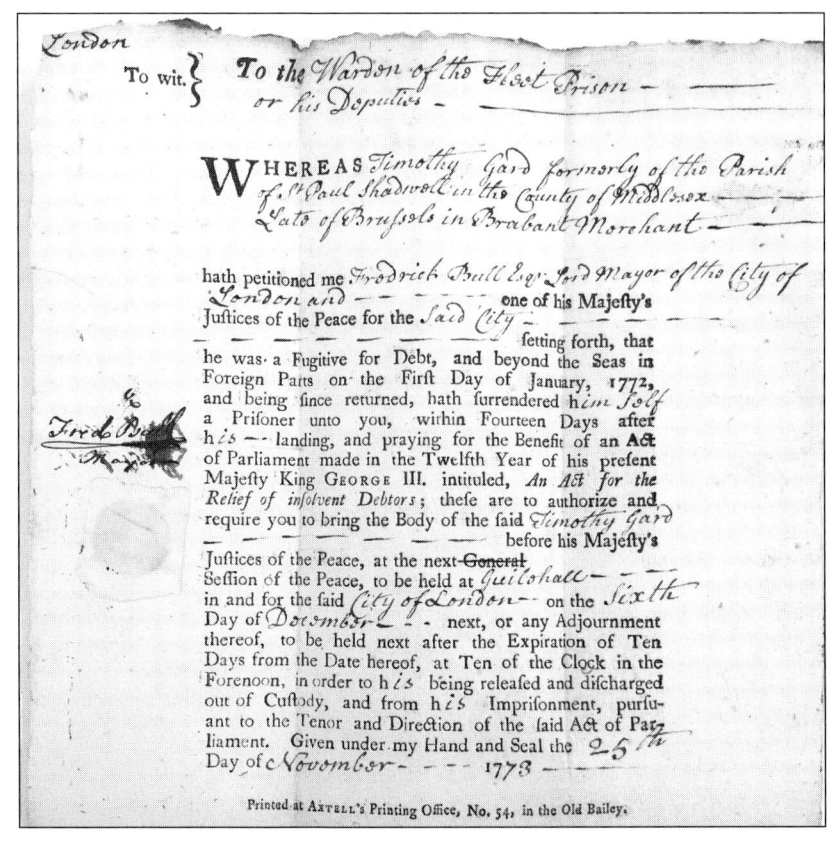

Debtors' schedule, 25 November 1773, relating to Thomas Gard, a fugitive returned from Brussels.

and from his Imprisonment, pursuant to the Tenor and Direction of the said Act of Parlaiment. Given under my Hand and Seal the 25th Day of November ~~~~~ 1773 ~~~~~

RELEASE OF INSOLVENT DEBTORS IN MIDDLESEX

Records of the Middlesex Sessions include records relating to prisoners for debt who were seeking to be discharged from prisons in Middlesex under the various Acts of Parliament. Prisoners applied from Newgate, Whitechapel Prison, Westminster Gatehouse, St Katherine's by the Tower (1671–1748), Stepney Gaol in Wellclose Square (1748 only), the Dean and Chapter of St Paul's (1671–1678 only) and the Duchy of Lancaster (1679 only).

| Debtors' schedules | 1671, 1678–1679, 1690–1692, 1737–1812 | MJ/SD/001-047 |

The records within MJ/SD/001-047 consist of several documents within a bundle, each one corresponding to a separate year and which run chronologically. The records can include petitions, lists of creditors, summons to creditors, orders to Keepers of prisons to bring the debtors to the Justices, lists of prisoners, orders of discharge and schedules of effects. It is possible to search for individual names using LMA's computerized catalogues.

RELEASE OF INSOLVENT DEBTORS IN SOUTHWARK

The Marshalsea and King's (Queen's) Bench prisons and Horsemonger Lane (Surrey County) Gaol were all situated in Southwark, in Surrey. Prisoners for debt who were seeking to be discharged from these prisons under the various Acts of Parliament therefore made their applications to the Surrey Quarter Sessions, with records now held at the Surrey History Centre in Woking.

| Debtors' Appearance Books | 1691–1798 | QS3/2/1-13 |
| Debtor Prisoners' Books | 1760–1811 | QS3/2/15-52-55-67 |

Debtors' Appearance Books, 1691–1798, QS3/2/1-13 give the session and justices before whom the insolvent debtors appeared followed by a list of the debtors dealt with at the session and the action taken. Many were not discharged as they had not supplied the necessary schedule of goods. Occasionally more information is given, such as: the regiments or ships joined by debtors as a condition of their release, or the substitute they provided; the name of the creditor; the name of the creditor to whom the debtor's goods were assigned; the reason why the debtor remained in custody; in which gaol a debtor was being held or if he was a fugitive.

Example: Debtors' Appearance Books, 1776.
Example from Debtors' Appearance Books 1776 relating to William Gray.

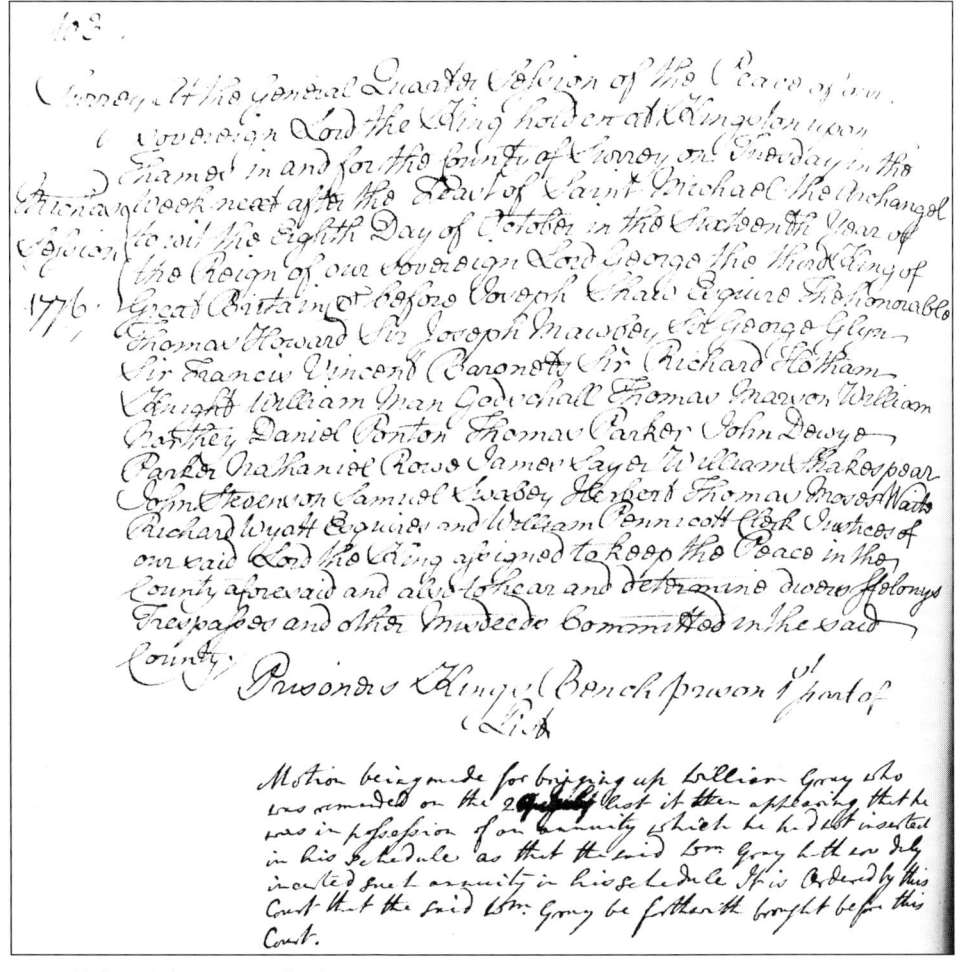

Debtors' Appearance Book.

Surrey
Mich~as Session 1776
At the General Quarter Session of the Peace of our sovereign Lord the King holden at Kingston upon Thames in and for the County of Surrey on Tuesday in the week next after the Feast of Saint Michael the Archangel to wit the Eighth Day of October in the Sixteenth year of the Reign of our sovereign Lord George the third King of Great Britain &c before … Justices of Our said Lord the King assigned to keep the Peace in the County aforesaid and also to hear and determine divers Felonys Trespasses and other Misdeeds Committed in the said County

Prisoners Kings Bench Prison 1st part of List
Motion being made for bringing up William Gray who was remanded on the 29 July list it then appearing that he was in possession of an annuity which he had not inserted in his schedule as that the said Wm Gray hath in July inserted such annuity in his schedule It is Ordered by this Court that the said Wm Gray be further brought before this Court.

The Debtor Prisoners' Books, 1760–1811, QS3/2/15-67 were lists submitted to the Quarter Sessions by keepers of the prisons in which the debtors were held. The lists were usually divided into two parts: the prisoners named in the first were those who were 'really and truly prisoners in actual custody', while the prisoners in the second part were those who had been committed since that date, had been discharged or had died, or had been removed to another prison. The lists are arranged alphabetically by debtor and the name of the creditor(s) is given.

Example: Debtor Prisoners' Books, 1773.

Alphabetical List of the Prisoners in the New Gaol
Southwark in the County of Surrey Pursuant to a late Act of parliament
Made for the Relief of Insolvent Debtors &c ~~~~~

Prisoners Names	When Committed	At Whose Suit
Aistrop John	5th October 1773	A warrant for £1. 5^s. 0^d for the Mentenance Cost and Charges of a Bastard Child to the parish officers of Saint Mary Lambeth
Burch Thomas	16th November 1773	Thomas Smith
Bateley Stephen	26th November 1773	Barnard Ogden

Chapter 9

COUNTY DEBTORS

Outside London, cases of debt would have been heard locally, in one of the courts of the relevant county. Most would have been brought before the Justices of the Peace at the Quarter Sessions, or possibly at one of the many Courts of Requests or, from 1846, at a County Court. In many of the ancient towns there were other local courts which had existed in earlier centuries and had survived through to Victorian times. But there was no national system. Many counties also had their own civil courts where debt cases may have been heard.

FIND-AN-ARCHIVE
Discovering what records survive at a local level requires research. The surest way of identifying local archives, record offices and libraries, any of which may hold records relating to debtors, is to use Find-an-archive, provided by The National Archives.

Find-an-archive allows searches to be made by location or keyword, specifically for information on the record offices themselves as opposed to details of the records they hold. In all, over 2,500 archives across the UK are included. To find an archive in the UK you can use the search box, click on the map or select from a list of UK regions and counties. The search results will show you contact information for the archive; brief information about the archive's collection; and a map showing the location of the archive.

The National Archives Discovery 'Advanced Search' also has

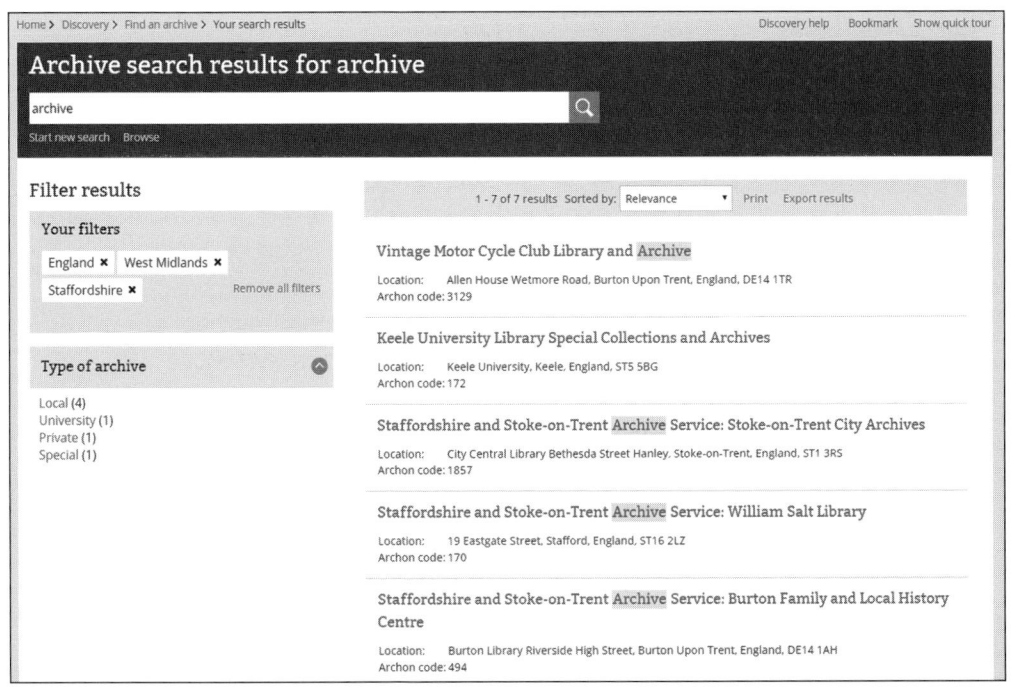

Find-an-archive screenshot.

the option to 'Search other archives' for more detailed information on their holdings. However, the catalogues that were uploaded to Discovery are now several years out-of-date. Nevertheless, this option can be a good starting point for discovering the whereabouts of record series held locally, although it is always safest then to refer to the current catalogue on the record office's own website.

As there are no certainties in how any collection or document may be described, be prepared to search under several possible keywords: 'debt', 'debtor', 'debtors', 'insolvency' as examples. Some may allow the use of wildcards, so debt* may produce all references to the first three, but not all online catalogues offer this option. More general terms such as Quarter Sessions may also be necessary.

TRIAL
Quarter Sessions
Keepers or conservators of the peace had been periodically appointed from 1285, but their powers were limited. From 1362, local gentry and noblemen acted as judges in their own counties. Known as Justices of the Peace, they held courts four times a year, which became known as Quarter Sessions or Quarter Sessions of the Peace. On the whole, they dealt with the less serious criminal cases on behalf of the Crown: cases involving such matters as poaching, vagrancy, assault and debt; without a jury at petty sessions, or with a jury at Quarter Sessions.

Under the Insolvent Debtors' Relief Act 1748, lists of debtors were presented to Quarter Sessions, while debtors themselves had to deliver schedules of their real and personal estate, all with a view to their discharge.

Courts of Requests
The predecessors of the modern County Courts were the Courts of Requests that had gradually been established in the 150 years before 1846. They were local tribunals providing a cheap alternative to seeking redress at the courts at Westminster. The origin of the Court of Requests in London dates to the reign of Henry VIII, but it was not until 1604 that it was given statutory recognition as a court. It took until 1688 for the first Courts of Requests to be established outside the City of London, in Newcastle upon Tyne, Bristol and Gloucester. Between 1748 and 1800 Parliament passed fifty-one Acts establishing these types of courts in various parts of Britain.

By 1840 there were 403 Courts of Requests in England and Wales, but they did not have a uniform constitution and jurisdiction and their distribution was uneven. Radnorshire had five courts, equating to one per 5,000 people, while at the other extreme, Cumberland had only two courts serving 178,000 people.

During the 1820s and 1830s, Henry Brougham and other politicians attempted to establish a national system of local civil courts. It was not until 1846 that an Act for the more easy Recovery of Small Debts and Demands in England received its Royal Assent.

County Courts

With abolition of the Courts of Requests, from 1846 County Courts were established to provide a national system for small debt recovery. England and Wales were divided into sixty districts in which one or more courts would operate. Each district was to have a judge who would be a barrister with at least seven years' experience. He would hear pleas of personal actions where the debt or damage claimed was not more than £20, but this rose to £50 in 1850.

Although the Court of Requests as a legal entity had been abolished, the jurisdiction of the new national County Court system was similar enough to its predecessor for many of the purpose-built Courts of Requests buildings to evolve into County Courts. For instance, Southwark Court of Requests became Southwark County Court in 1847 and remained in use until the early twentieth century. However, the new court system soon led to the creation of a new uniform building type, due to the design of the court buildings being managed centrally by a Surveyor of County Courts until the abolition of the post in 1870.

PRISONS

Although matters had improved a little in the major London prisons by the late eighteenth century, conditions in local gaols, on the whole, remained bad. In 1782 it was discovered that of twenty-two debtors in Gloucester Castle, only seven slept in beds; the rest lay on straw. In 1812, James Neild reported that in Dorchester criminal prisoners were regularly allowed coal to heat their common room, but debtors were only allowed it in the most severe weather. Many county and other gaols had a separate debtors' side, but for prisons, as with local courts, there was no national system or standard.

In December 1843, Mr Weale was horrified by what he found in the Birmingham Debtors' Prison. He described it as the 'den of wretchedness'. The prison, he explained, was formerly an ordinary dwelling house and had twenty-two 'poor creatures', including one woman who had been provided with straw bedding and a ten-inch wide sleeping space.

There are some records relating to county debtors' prisons held at The National Archives:

- Register of debtors received in Lincolnshire county gaol between 1810 and 1822 in PCO 2/309. The register is possibly the fair copy written around 1822 and gives details of 1,200 prisoners, including their names, their debts and the courts from which they came.
- Many people imprisoned for debt in Shrewsbury gaol in PCOM 2/39.
- Many people imprisoned for debt in Lancaster gaol in PCOM 2/440.
- Applications for Release to the Justices of the Peace from imprisoned insolvent prisoners in Cheshire, 1760–1830 in CHES 10.
- Records for the prison attached to Court of Requests for the town of Birmingham and hamlet of Deritend, in HO 45/775, contains several interesting descriptions of conditions in the debtors' prison in Birmingham in the 1840s.
- Registers of petitions of country prisoners are in B 6. These can include petitions, depositions etc. and discharges.

REPORTS OF THE INSPECTORS OF PRISONS OF GREAT BRITAIN

The Reports were first published in 1836 and included very detailed reports of all the prisons in Great Britain. These include a great deal of information on debtors' prisons or other gaols where debtors were imprisoned. For example, the Digest section of the *Fifteenth Report* (1850) shows that in the course of the year 1849, 8,519 people were imprisoned for debt, 8,255 men and 264 women. There are detailed tables for each county, so for Devon there were 136 men and four women in six different prisons – the majority, 100, being in the Devon County Debtors' Prison.

The Inspectors' reports were very full, although many of their comments were extremely subjective. Again, in the 1850 Report, the Inspector of the Lancaster County Gaol noted that his recommendations, made the previous year, had not been acted upon. These were:

1. As soon as practicable, after the withdrawal of the prisoners from Manchester, the prison to be discontinued for male criminal prisoners.
2. The debtors to be classified, as far as practicable, according to character, conduct, the circumstances under which they are committed, and the question whether or not they maintain themselves; and all the male debtors, except the best class, to occupy the northern part of the Crown side of the prison; the best class to be put in a portion of the southern side.
3. The debtors who are maintained by the county to have a regular and moderate dietary of cooked food, and no cooking to be permitted in the rooms of these debtors. The rule also which forbids such debtors from having any additional supplies from without to be strictly enforced.
4. In order to prevent the introduction of spirits, tobacco, and other forbidden articles, visitors to the lower classes of debtors to be placed under the same restrictions as visitors to criminal prisoners.
5. The hours for visiting debtors to be reduced to three per day.
6. A time and place to be appointed for drinking fermented liquor, and no fermented liquor to be allowed to go into any other part of the prison. An officer to be present, but no debtor who has not purchased any liquor to be permitted to be there; the time not to extend beyond a quarter of an hour.

7. No debtor to be allowed to have any part of the county bedding if he brings to any bedding of his own. Bolsters to be added to the bedding provided for debtors.

8. The debtors, like other prisoners, to be prohibited from whistling, singing, or otherwise disturbing the order of the prison; and no such games as skittles to be allowed among them.

9. Some of the cells on the females' side to be prepared for the separate confinement of prisoners, according to the provisions of the 2 and 3 Vict. c.56, s.4; and as a general rule every female criminal prisoner to be either in a separate cell or in a class under immediate and constant superintendence.

10. The hammocks, which are inconveniently high, to be lowered. (The work could be done by prisoners.)

11. The females' side of the prison to be lighted with gas; and the prisoners to be required to rise not later than at six all the year around, and not to be allowed to go to bed before nine at night.

12. As far as practicable each prisoner to be required to perform a daily task equal to ten hours' fair labour.

13. The officers to wear a uniform; among other reasons, in order that they may be at once distinguished from prisoners.

The reports frequently mention the resistance of some debtors to seek release from imprisonment, preferring to remain where they were. In 1850, the Inspector of the Hampshire County Gaol noted:

> … the extraordinary fact of one debtor having been confined in this county gaol for 36 years. I inquired very minutely into his case, and found his prolonged detention owing entirely to his own obstinacy. I made use of every argument to induce him to take the necessary but simple steps for his own release, but in reply to my question as to whether he would take the benefit of the Act he replied, 'I will not'.

County Debtors

> In the Oxford County Gaol and House of Correction it was noted that:
>
> One debtor, I regret to say a clergyman of the Church of England, has been here for several years, and does not appear to contemplate the taking any steps to obtain his discharge.

RECORDS EXAMPLES

Apart from some King's Bench and Marshalsea Prison records on Ancestry, few others relating to debtors are included in the records provided by the several online providers. Gloucester County Gaol, Debtors' Registers 1834–54, 1868–79 are also available on Ancestry.

There is no consistency in the type of record that may survive in county and other record offices around the country. These may include lists of debtors or just a single reference to one. They can include private papers formerly with solicitors' offices, prison registers, petitions under the many Insolvent Debtors' Acts, ecclesiastical records, records created under the Poor Laws, and many others. Therefore, examples from just a few county and other record offices must suffice to indicate the range of material that can be found on insolvent debtors outside London.

Wiltshire

The online catalogue for Wiltshire and Swindon History Centre, in Chippenham, includes 851 references to 'debt*' – the wildcard * means that the search would include debt, debts, debtor and debtors. There were twenty hits for debtor* and just thirteen for debt* +prison.

The Wiltshire County Court sat in Devizes and Wilton, with the majority of the surviving papers being in the Quarter Sessions archives (A1/850). The catalogue entry gives more detailed information on the collection.

However, Wilton, like many boroughs around the country, had its own small debts court, and many plaints (actions for debt) for the

Reference	A1/850
Level	Item
Title	Pleas in the County Court, 1636-7, 1647-64 (16 files; c2000 docts). These concern actions of debt mainly for loans of money, but also for goods and services purchased. There are some writs from the sheriff to the bailiff of the appropriate Hundred to distrain the goods of debtors. There are references on the pleas to folios of a record book or books not extant. The court sat at Devizes and Wilton. 1-2 . 1636-1637. 3. 1646-1661 (3); 4. 1649-1653. 5. 1650-1659 (2). 6. 1650-1657 (2). 7. 1652-1660 (2). 8. 1654-1658. 9. 1655-1662. 10. 1656-1662. 11. 1659-1662. 12. 1659-1661. 13. 1661-1663. 14. 1662-1664. 15. 1652-1658. 16. 1661 writs.
Date	1636-1664
Related Material	G25/1/52-53. These were added to the archives of Wilton Borough presumably when the Quarter Sessions archives were kept in the town.

Catalogue entry for Pleas in the County Court.

years 1636–1637, 1650–1661, are included in the Borough's archive (G25/1/52-53). In all, there are some 3,000 plaints: the names of parties and the place the debt was incurred are given; where judgement is given, the presiding magistrates signed. For example, in 1673 Mathew Allen sought payment from William Nicholson of 33s for a debt at Christian Malford for 3¼ virgates of black cloth worth 13s, and ¼ virgate of tawny cotton worth 10s.

Other records held at the Wiltshire and Swindon History Centre are gaolers' lists of debtors imprisoned in the County Gaol at Fisherton Anger, petitions for discharge and schedules of prisoners' real and personal estate, delivered to Quarter Sessions under the Insolvent Debtors Relief Act of 1724–5, 1724-1781 (A1/120).

In 1748, the creditors of Edward Reeves petitioned the Quarter Sessions for his assets to be assigned to their representative, Henry Pearce.

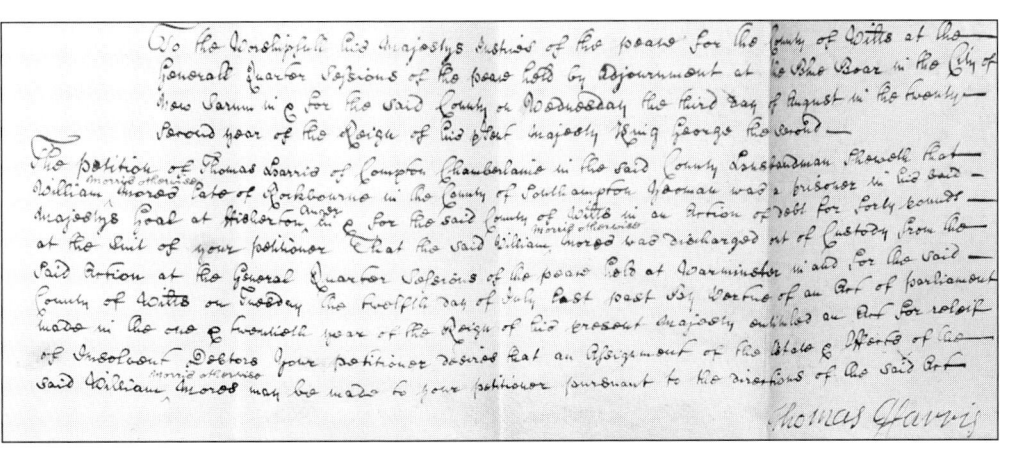

Petition from the creditors of Edward Reeves to the Quarter Sessions, 1748.

To the Right Worshipfull the Justices of the Peace for the County of Wilts at the Quarter Sessions Assembled.

We whose Names are hereunto Subscribed being the Major part of the Creditors of Edward Reeves who was Discharged out of the custody of the last General Quarter Sessions of the Peace held at Warminster in and for the said County By Virtue of an Act of Parliament made in the 21st Year of the Reign of his present Majesty King George the Second Intitled An Act for the Relief of Insolvent Debtors who have Applied for the same Do most humbly request & desire that you the said Justices will be pleased to direct and appoint the Clerk of the peace for the said County to make and Assignment of all the Estate Right Title and Interest and Trust of the said Edward Reeves of in and unto Such Reall Estate as well Copy or Customary hold as Freehold And all Such Personal Estate Debts and Effects as are mentioned and Contained in the Schedule delivered in by the said Edward Reeves in Pursuance of the said Act To Henry Pearce of Bulford in the sd County Blacksmith In Trust for himself and the rest of the Creditors of the said Edward Reeves According to the Tenor and Effect of the said Act

[signed by the creditors]

Also, for 1748, the Series includes a list of debtors held in the county gaol at Fisherton Anger.

Wiltshire To Wit	A True Exact and Perfect List Alphabetically of the Names of all and every person or persons who upon the First day of January in the Year of our Lord One Thousand Seven Hundred and Forty seven were and now are Actually Prisoner or Prisoners in the Custody of Edward Holdaway Keeper of his Majesties Gaol at Fisherton Anger in and For the County Aforesaid Upon any process whatsoever for or by Reason of any Debt Damages Costs Sum or Sums of Money and of the Dates of the Warrants to the times when Charged in Custody together with the Name or Names of the Person or Persons at whose respective Suits Such Prisoners are Detained Dated the First ~~~~ day of July 1748					
Prisoners Names	On what Actions Charged	At Whose Suit Charged	Date of the Warrant	When Charged	In what Sums Charged	
Jane Ashton widow	Latitat	Thomas Neale	25th November 1746	5th December 1746	£ s d 300. 0. 0	
John Abbott	Execution	Peter Hawker Esqr	2 December 1746	10 December 1746	108. 0. 0 Discharged X	X
Richard Compton	Latitat	Thomas Warren	2 June 1747	17 June 1747	132. 0. 0 Discharged X	X
Mary Crew	Latitat	Robert Holmes & George Wheatley	16 June 1747	24 June 1747	40. 0. 0 Discharged X	X
[etc.]						

Other records concerning debt and debtors are found in the Bishop of Salisbury's Court of Pleas:

- Cognovits, 1811–1816, D1/29/11. These were acknowledgements by the defendant of his debt to the plaintiff.
- Affidavits for debt, 1807–22, 1744-47, D1/29/3

County Debtors

Prisoners held for debt etc. in Fisherton Anger Gaol on 1 January 1748.

In the 1861 Census of the County Gaol at Fisherton Anger, three inmates are described as 'Sheriffs Debtor' (RG9/1315 f.43 p.30) including two clergymen, one aged eighty-six:

Charles J Coleman	Sheriffs debtor	Widr	86	Clergyman	Do Basingstoke
George London	do	Mar	56	do	Oxon Oxford
George Powell	do	do	47	Butcher	Somerset Bath

Dorset

The online catalogue for Dorset Record Office in Dorchester produces 669 results for a search for 'debt*. A search for 'debtor*' reduces the number of hits to fifty; and a search for debt* *and* prison produces just eleven results.

Many of the resulting entries are papers relating to named individuals. Often these are not in debtors' records *per se*, but individuals noted in miscellaneous categories of document as being debtors or being confined in a debtors' prison.

For instance, there is a settlement examination for Whitechurch Canonicorum Parish (PE-WCC/OV/4/1/3), where the examinant, George Grinter, is described as being a debtor:

> The Examination of George Grinter a Debtor now confined in the county Gaol at Dorchester in the said county of Dorset, ~~~~~~~~~~~ taken on Oath, before us ~~~~~~~~~~
> his Majesty's Justices of the Peace for the county of Dorset, this ninth day of September 1815 ~~~~~

Another example is from a 1764 deed relating to lands at West Knoyle, Wiltshire (D-FFO/22/10):

> Michaelmas Term in the Fiftieth Year of the Reign of King George the third
> To wit, James Brown Complains of George Grandy being in the Custody of the Marshal of The Marshalsea of our Lord the King before the King himself for this to wit …

Other records relate mainly to Dorchester's present prison on the site in North Square. The building work was completed in 1795 and generally prisoners were detained in cells, except debtors who were confined in dormitories and had access to a day room.

Records of Dorchester Prison include a very detailed Debtors' Register, 1793–1842 (NG-PR/1/D/4/1) which includes: prisoners' names; parish; age; trade; marital status; no. of children; writ from what court issued; dates of writ, warrant and when brought to prison; amount of debt; plaintiff's name; how and when discharged. The vast majority had been tried in one of the central Common Law Courts: Common Pleas, King's Bench or Exchequer.

Surrey
Many counties may have published guides to the Quarter Sessions and other court records. For example, for Surrey there is a *Guide to archives and other collections of documents relating to Surrey: Quarter Sessions with other records of the Justices of the Peace* (Surrey Record Society, Number XXXII, 1931). Caution is required when using such published material as the accuracy and completeness of such volumes may be out-of-date.

County Debtors

> *PRISONERS' BOOKS, CALENDARS AND RETURNS.*
> *Books, Insolvent Debtors*, MS. volumes, bound and indexed.
> *1737–1798.*
>
> 1.—1737, 1743, 1748, 1755. 7.—1776–1778.
> 2.—1761–1763.   8.—1777–1778.
> 3.—1765–1767.   9.—1781–1783.
> 4.—1769–1771.   10.—1794–1796.
> 5.—1772–1774.   11.—1797–1798.
> 6.—1774–1776.
>
> *Books, Insolvent Debtors*, MS. volumes, unbound and indexed.
> *1778–1815 (L.N. 273).*
>
> 1.—1778–1780.   5.—1804–1805.   9.—1812.
> 2.—1797.   6.—1806–1808.   10.—1811–1813.
> 3.—1801.   7.—1809–1811.   11.—1812–1813.
> 4.—1801–1802.   8.—1811–1812.   12.—1814–1815.
>
> (With two original Schedules as required by the Act of 54, Geo. III., for John Lonsdale, 1813, and Noah Edward Lewis, 1813).

Extract from Guide to archives and other collections of documents relating to Surrey: Quarter Sessions with other records of the Justices of the Peace. (Surrey Record Society, Number XXXII, 1931)

The first section relates to Sessions held at Kingston County Hall and now held at Surrey History Centre with the reference QS3/2-11, to which additional returns have since been identified, QS3/12-13. The second refers to those held at Newington Sessions House in 1931: these cannot now be identified and were probably destroyed when the Sessions House was bombed during the Second World War.

In Surrey, pleas of debt were heard by the Court of Record in Kingston, also known as the Saturday Court. This had the power to commit debtors to the town gaol, known as the Stockhouse – a separate debtors' prison was not built until 1829. The court sat on Saturdays and cases were heard by a bench consisting of the Recorder of Kingston and two of the Bailiffs (magistrates).

Most records relating to Surrey debtors are therefore to be found as part of Kingston History Centre's collections, at Guildhall, Kingston upon Thames. The major relevant collection is the Court of Record Books, KE1.

It is therefore essential to consider the archive collections in local or borough record offices, in addition to the major collections held in the county record offices. Making initial searches on Discovery – although the information may be out-of-date – is still probably the best way of discovering the existence of such collections.

Chapter 10

BANKRUPTCY

In the eighteenth and nineteenth century, there were about 15,000 bankruptcies recorded each year in England and Wales. Some form of law covering bankrupts can be traced back to ancient Babylon, but in England, the first recognized legislation was introduced during the reign of Henry VIII with the 1542 Statute of Bankrupts:

An Acte againste suche persones as doo make Bankrupte 1542
Whereas divers and sundry persons craftily obtaining into their hands great substance of other mens goods, do suddenly flee to parts unknown, or keep their houses, not minding to pay or restore to any their creditors, their debts and duties, but at their own wills and pleasures consume the substance obtained by credit of other men, for their own pleasure and delicate living, against all reason, equity and good conscience:

I.

… the lord Chancellor … to order the same for true satisfaction and payment of the said creditors: that is to say, to every of the said creditors, a portion, rate and rate like, according to the quantity of their debts …

V.

… all goods, chattels, lands, tenements and debts of every such offender shall be by the order and direction of the said lords employed and distributed amongst his creditors equally and indifferently rate for rate, in the manner and form as is afore declared.

It was the first statute under English law dealing with bankruptcy or insolvency. The Act reflected the deep-rooted belief that people who could not pay their debts were criminals and required debtors to be imprisoned. Bankrupts were seen as crooks, and the 1542 Bankruptcy Act stated its aim to prevent 'crafty debtors' escaping the realm. Under the Act, estates of fraudulent debtors could be seized and divided among creditors without providing any relief for the bankrupt.

The 1542 Act introduced the principle of *pari passu* (proportional) distribution of losses among creditors. An insolvent person's possessions would be distributed among creditors in proportion to the debts owed. Initially, the administration of any bankruptcy proceedings was delegated to the Court of King's Bench or Court of Common Pleas, and occasionally to a member of the Privy Council. When creditors petitioned for a fiat or commission they had to prove they were owed money. The 1542 Act wasn't repealed until 1825, under the Bankrupts Act that year.

Bankruptcy was therefore the process whereby a court official declared a qualifying debtor bankrupt, took over his property and distributed it to the creditors in proportion to what they were owed. The word 'bankruptcy' is formed from the Latin *bancus* (a bench or table), and *ruptus* (broken). It was from these benches that the early bankers undertook their business at markets and fairs. If their business failed, an old Italian custom called for the breaking of these benches, showing they were no longer dealing.

In Evelyn Waugh's 1945 *Brideshead Revisited*, Edward Ryder, commenting on his son Charles's difficult financial situation, remarks dryly:

Hard up? Penurious? Distressed? Embarrassed? Stoney broke? On the rocks? In Queer Street? – Your cousin Melchior was imprudent with his investments and got into a very queer street – worked his passage to Australia before the mast.

It is probable that 'Queer' is a corruption of 'Carey', from Carey Street, where the bankruptcy courts moved to from Westminster in the 1840s.

It was the Bankruptcy Act of 1571 that first allowed a bankrupt to settle his debts by an equitable distribution of his remaining assets through independent commissioners of bankrupts.

An Act Touching Orders for Bankrupts 1571
Forasmuch as notwithstanding the statute made against bankrupts in the thirty-fourth year of the reign of our sovereign lord King Henry the Eighth, those kind of persons have and do still increase into great and excessive numbers, and are like more to do, if some better provision be made for the repression of them, and do a plain declaration to be made and set forth, who is and ought to be taken and deemed for a bankrupt:

II.

That the lord chancellor ... shall have full power and authority by commission under the great seal of England, to name, assign and appoint such wise and honest discreet persons as to him shall seem good ...

... or otherwise to order the same for true satisfaction and payment of the said creditors; that is to say, to every of the said creditors a portion, rate and rate like, according to the quantity of his or their debts ...

Before the 1571 Act, cases were mainly brought before the King's Bench or the Court of Common Pleas. Bankrupts could be any debtors involved in economic activity, and there was little distinction between the fraudulent and the merely unfortunate.

The Act of 1571 also empowered the Lord Chancellor, upon complaint in writing against a bankrupt, to appoint Commissioners of Bankrupts. The Commissioners were independent assessors who would decide whether a debtor was eligible for bankruptcy proceedings.

That bankrupts were subject to the total will of their creditors, is well represented by Shylock demanding his 'pound of flesh' in Shakespeare's *Merchant of Venice*:

Duke: How shalt thou hope for mercy, rendering none?
Shylock: What judgment shall I dread, doing no wrong? You have among you many a purchas'd slave, Which, like your asses and your dogs and mules, You use in abject and in slavish parts, Because you bought them; shall I say to you 'Let them be free, marry them to your heirs? Why sweat they under burdens? let their beds Be made as soft as yours, and let their palates Be season'd with such viands? You will answer 'The slaves are ours.' So do I answer you: The pound of flesh which I demand of him Is dearly bought; 'tis mine, and I will have it. If you deny me, fie upon your law! There is no force in the decrees of Venice.
I stand for judgment: answer; shall I have it?

Bankruptcy proceedings commenced when creditors petitioned for a commission of bankruptcy – or 'fiat' from 1832. If they were able to prove they were owed money, commissioners and a provisional assignee were appointed.

Creditors appeared before the Commissioners or a Master in Chancery where the debts were assessed, and the claims noted. If there was substantial disagreement, the Lord Chancellor may have become involved. Notices would be placed in the *London Gazette*, and possibly in local newspapers, advising of meetings for the granting of commissions or fiats, the appointment of assignees, declaration of dividends, and any annulment of commissions or fiats.

Evidence could be sought from anyone, from the creditors to friends, and even the debtor's spouse, about the debts and the financial position of the debtor. The creditors would then appoint assignees to assess the estate and value the assets and distribute them as dividends. If everything was in order the Commissioners declared the debtor bankrupt. Further notices were then placed in the *London Gazette* with a list of potential creditors and the date of meetings.

The provisional trustee would be replaced by a permanent one, agreed on by the creditors, and the Commissioner then transferred the bankrupt's estate to him for valuation, establishing and collecting debts and continuing to run the business. With the creditors' consent, the assets could be sold by auction: if necessary, the assignee could sell everything before the distribution of the dividends. Once a balance sheet had been produced, the final examination was made, and a statement drawn up. Once the balance sheet and statement were accepted by a sufficient number of creditors (75–80 percent), the creditors signed another petition to discharge the bankrupt, who was given a Certificate of Conformity allowing him to recommence trading if he so wished – this may have taken many years.

A more benevolent approach was developed under the Bankrupts Act of 1705 (An Act to prevent Fraud frequently committed by Bankrupts). The Lord Chancellor was given power to discharge bankrupts once disclosure of all assets and various procedures had been fulfilled. Following pressure from traders, led by the novelist Daniel Defoe, who had suffered financially as a result of overseas war, who saw little reason to enter into any compromise or disclose their assets, it became possible for a discharged bankrupt to recommence trading.

Even by the nineteenth century the rules surrounding bankruptcy, as with debt, were complex. There was always a clear distinction between debt and bankruptcy – the insolvent debtor and the bankrupt – and it is important to understand the difference between the two. Because the right to bankruptcy was such a valuable asset, it was limited to persons the law considered to be traders.

Until 1842, the legal status of being a bankrupt, and therefore able to pay off creditors and be discharged of all outstanding debts, was confined to traders owing more than £100 – the emphasis being on 'trader'.

Debtors who were not traders did not qualify to become bankrupt but were given the status of 'insolvent debtor'. By the eighteenth century 'traders' included most skilled craftsmen such as butchers, ship's carpenters, master tailors and brickmakers, but not innkeepers and ordinary tailors. Notably, farmers were specifically excluded from this regulation. Those debtors who were not eligible to claim bankruptcy remained insolvent, subject to common law and, if their creditors wished, were confined indefinitely in prison, responsible for their debts but unable to pay them. As has been seen in earlier chapters, they remained subject to common law proceedings and indefinite imprisonment if their creditors so wished.

Because bankruptcy was more attractive than spending a few years in gaol, debtors sometimes pretended to be traders, and gave misleading descriptions of their occupations – dealer and chapman (salesman) was very common. From 1861 all insolvent debtors were allowed to apply for bankruptcy.

By the early nineteenth century, attitudes were changing. From 1822, those who were owed money could petition the Lord Chancellor for a Commission of Bankruptcy. The Commissioners were independent assessors who made the decision as to whether a person was eligible for bankruptcy, or not. They would then oversee the distribution of the assets to the bankrupt's creditors. When enough creditors were satisfied with the way the assessors had managed proceedings, they had to sign a request for a Certificate of Conformity. This meant that they were happy that the bankrupt had met all the legal requirements. From 1849 to 1861 there were three types of certificates:

- Where the bankrupts were blameless
- Where some blame could be attributed
- Where it was entirely the bankrupts' fault

The Bankrupts (England) Act 1825 allowed people to start proceedings for their own bankruptcy, in agreement with creditors. Previously only creditors could start the proceedings. Bankruptcy proceedings agreed between creditors and debtor also occurred when a trader filed a declaration of insolvency in the office of the Chancellor's Secretary of Bankrupts, which was then advertised in the *London Gazette*. The advertised declaration supported a commission in bankruptcy to be issued. The new law decreed that no commission grounded on this act of bankruptcy was to be 'deemed invalid by reason of such declaration having been concerted or agreed upon between the bankrupt and any creditor or other person'.

COURTS OF BANKRUPTCY

The system of handling bankruptcy established in the sixteenth century remained virtually unchanged until 1831, when the Bankruptcy Court (England) Act established a special court in London, the London Court of Bankruptcy. At the same time, a Court of Review was established to hear appeals from the Bankruptcy Court, but this was abolished in 1847 when appeals were directed to the Court of Chancery. The main function of the Bankruptcy Court was to give creditors an opportunity to petition the Lord Chancellor for a Commission of Bankruptcy to investigate the alleged bankruptcy and to try to recover due debts. If the debts had been recovered the bankrupt would receive a Certificate of Conformity.

Until 1869, the Court of Bankruptcy was administered by two judges of the Chancery Division, with bankruptcy registrars who dealt with the routine cases in London, and County Court justices who dealt with provincial cases.

In 1842, District Bankruptcy Courts were established for areas outside of London – sometimes defined as a twenty-mile radius from the centre – and provincial cases were heard locally. From 1869 their jurisdiction passed to the County Court (they had some jurisdiction since 1847), although they could be transferred to the London Court by special resolution of the creditors. Surviving records will probably be held in the relevant local county record office. Details of what is available locally may be found by searching relevant catalogues – the keyword search terms 'bankrupt' and 'bankruptcy', or 'bankrupt*' should all be tried.

The Bankruptcy Act 1869 was passed allowing all people, rather than just traders, to file for bankruptcy. Creditors who were owed more than £50 could petition for bankruptcy proceedings. Cases in London were dealt with by the London Court of Bankruptcy, the records of which are held at The National Archives. London was defined as the City and the areas covered by the metropolitan County Courts of Bloomsbury, Bow, Brompton, Clerkenwell, Lambeth, Marylebone, Southwark, Shoreditch, Westminster and Whitechapel.

From 1883, the London Court of Bankruptcy was incorporated into the Supreme Court as the High Court of Justice in Bankruptcy. It subsequently became responsible for the additional metropolitan County Court areas of Barnet, Brentford, Edmonton, Wandsworth, West London and Willesden. Bankruptcy petitions were only to be presented to the High Court if the debtor had resided or carried on business within the London Bankruptcy District for six months, if he was not resident in England or if the petitioning creditor could not identify where he lived. Otherwise, the High Court judges would refer cases to the County Courts, or from 1884 to the Board of Trade.

A High Court judge could, however, transfer any bankruptcy case to or from a County Court. After 1883, official receivers supervised by the Bankruptcy Department of the Board of Trade took over responsibility for the administration of the bankrupt's estate once a court had determined the fact of bankruptcy and made a receiving order. Its records therefore cover cases dealt with by both the High Court and the County Courts.

RECORDS
As with insolvent debtors, often the best place to start research is with the *London Gazette*. All records held at The National Archives

Bankruptcy

refer to England and Wales only. There are no records before 1710 and from then they survive only patchily at first. London records are complete from 1821 and those for the rest of the country from 1832. Other sources make up many of the deficiencies. Most records are arranged alphabetically or indexed. Many distinguish between London and county records.

From 1842, records relating to bankruptcy cases outside London may be held by county record offices. After 1869, they should normally be held among the records of the County Courts, although sometimes the London Court of Bankruptcy could hear cases transferred from County Courts at creditors' request.

Early Commissions of Bankruptcy were enrolled on the Patent Rolls, C 66 and C 67. From the early eighteenth century, the surviving records of bankrupts and bankruptcy are comprised mainly of Case Files and various forms of register or Docket Books. Sometimes, records against individuals can be found in other courts: Chancery, Exchequer, King's Bench and Common Pleas.

Bankruptcy Case Files

Office of the Commissioners of Bankrupts and Court of Bankruptcy: Bankruptcy Commission Files	B 3	1753 to 1854
Court of Bankruptcy and successors: Proceedings under the Bankruptcy Acts	B 9	1832 to about 1970
Court of Bankruptcy: Proceedings under the Joint Stock Companies Acts, 1856 and 1857	B 10	1857–1863
Miscellaneous Exhibits	C 217	Early nineteenth century

The majority of Case Files have not survived. Those that do are within the records of the Office of the Commissioners of Bankrupts, its successors and the Court for the Relief of Insolvent Debtors. Over 5,800 Case Files are in the Files of Commissions of Bankrupts, dating

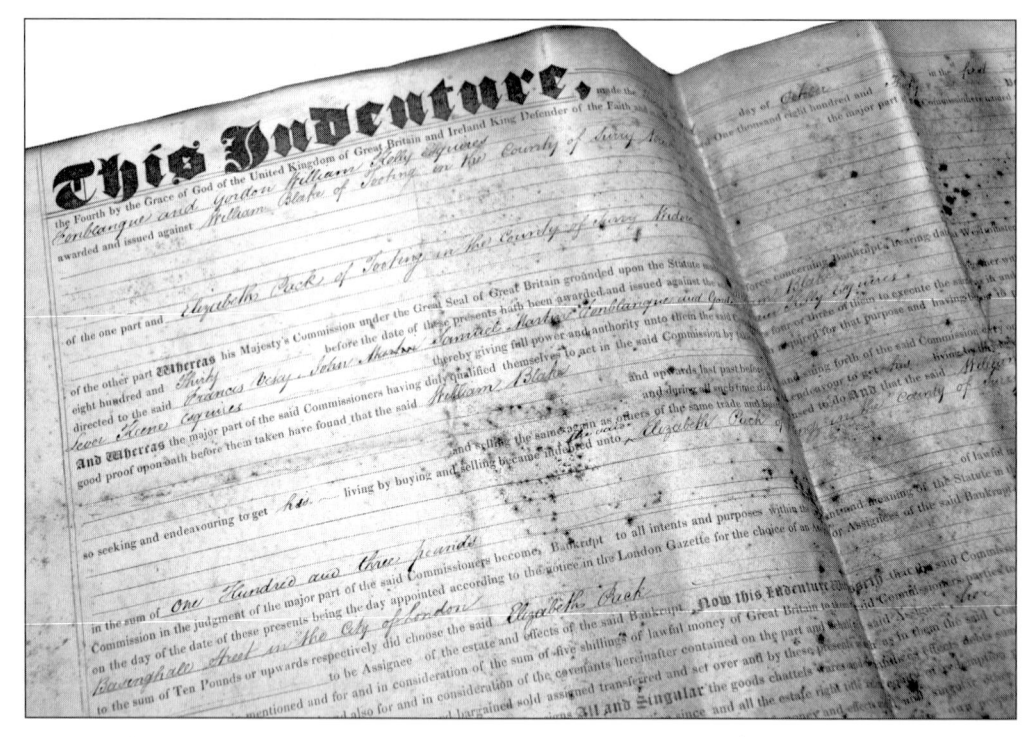

Example of document from the Case Book for William Blake of Tooting in the County of Surrey who owed Elizabeth Pack £103.0.0, 22 October 1830.

from 1753 to 1854, B 3, the majority between 1780 and 1842. These are searchable on Discovery by name, trade or occupation.

The Case File for William Blake, a brewer of Tooting, includes numerous copies of entries from the *London Gazette*, as well as official court documentation.

This Indenture made the Twenty second day of October in the first year of the Reign of our sovereign Lord William The forth by the Grace of God of the United Kingdom of Great Britain and Ireland King Defender of the Faith and in the year of out Lord One thousand eighth hundred Thirty
Between Francis Vesey John Samuel Martin Fontblanque and

Gordon William Kelly Esquires ~~~~~ the major part of the Commissioners named authorized and appointed in and by certain Commission of Bankrupt awarded and issued against William Blake of Tooting in the County of Surry Brewer of the one part and Elizabeth Pack of Tooting Widow
[etcetera]

Although some Commissioners of Bankrupts held their sittings in Guildhall, very few records survive among the archives of the City of London, held at London Metropolitan Archives, except for the Bankrupts books of Hallkeeper's office records, which record fees paid to the hallkeepers by the messengers to the Commissioners in Bankrupts (whose names are included) in respect of sittings 1793–1821 (CLA/040/07/009-025).

A second series commences in 1832 and continues to about 1970, B 9. From 1869, they relate mainly to London when the London Court of Bankruptcy was established. This second series includes over 1,700 cases to the year 2000, but with a thirty-year closure. This is a very small sample (less than 5 percent of Bankruptcy Case Files) and is arranged chronologically by date of filing of petition. These files may be one or more volumes: those for A.W. Carpenter, trading as the Charing Cross Bank, run to 152 volumes. Entries are searchable on Discovery by name and trade.

The Case File for Frederick Child provided full details of the claims made by the Deeds, leather merchants of Oxford Street:

The Bankruptcy Act, 1869
To the County Court of Surrey holden at Croydon
The Humble petition of John Simpkin Deed Martin Deed and Alfred Deed of 451 Oxford Street in the County of Middlesex leather merchants and copartners carrying on business under the style of John S Deed and Sons
That Frederick Child ~~~~~ of Dorking in the County of Surrey Glove & Gaiter Maker and Fell monger does not reside

or carry on business within the District of the London Bankruptcy Court and carries on business within the district of this Court, that is to say, at Dorking in the County of Surrey, That the said Frederick Child ~~~~~ is indebted to your Petitioners ~~~~ in the sum of one hundred and sixty nine pounds fourteen shillings and eight pence for goods sold and delivered by your petitioners to the said Frederick Child at his request between the first day of June and the 14th day of November 1872 ~~~~~

That your Petitioners do not nor doth any person or persons in their behalf hold any security on the Bankrupt's estate or on any part thereof for the payment of the said sum of one hundred and sixty nine pounds fourteen shillings and six pence ~~~~~

That the said Frederick Child ~~~~~ ~~~~~ has committed an Act of Bankruptcy within six months before the presentation of this petition.

That the Act of Bankruptcy committed him is that the said Frederick Child has filed in the prescribed manner in this Court a Declaration admitting his inability to pay his Debts. Your petitioners therefore humbly pray that on proof of the requisites in that Behalf, on the hearing of this petition, the said Frederick Child ~~~~~ may be adjudicated a Bankrupt And your Petitioner shall ever pray, &c.

Signed on the 5th day of   )   Alfred Deed
August 1873   )   for self a partner
[etcetera]

There are some further Case Files (under the Joint Stock Company Acts 1856–57) for 1857–1863, B 10. These are searchable on Discovery by Joint-Stock Company name.

Most surviving Case Files are extremely comprehensive and can run to several volumes, containing all the details and collected papers of the case: the numerous legal documents, newspaper cuttings, affidavits, debtor's balance sheets and possibly itemised creditors accounts. It is only if the Case File survives that there will be a copy of the original Petition for Bankruptcy.

Although these Case Files cover only a small percentage of all bankruptcy cases, nevertheless they are the place to start research, as the three Series B 3, B 9 and B 10 are indexed under various terms on Discovery.

C 217 contains a miscellany of exhibits in a few bankruptcy cases in the early nineteenth century

Bankruptcy Proceedings before 1869

If no Case File survives, then it will be necessary to resort to the other surviving record series. These Registers and Docket Books will only contain the briefest of details, but will at least confirm that a bankruptcy did take place and, if it was a country case, possibly allow searches in local archives, or in local or national newspapers, to be undertaken. Generally speaking, the records are arranged in chronological order and then by initial letter of surname of the bankrupt within each volume.

Office of the Commissioners of Bankrupts and Court of Bankruptcy: Bankruptcy Commission Docket Books	B 4/1–52	1710 to 1849
Registers of renewed Commissions of Bankruptcy	B 4/53–56	1743-1833
Office of the Commissioners of Bankrupts and successors: Order Books relating to Petitions against Declarations of Bankruptcy	B 1	1710-1877
Other administrative records	B 2, B 5–B 8, B 11–12	
General Docket Books, for the London District	B 6/99–117	1849 to 1869:
General Docket Books, for the Country District	B 6/118–124	1849 to 1869

County Court Docket Books	B 6/125–132	1861–1869
Declarations of insolvency: town and country	B 6/74–81	1825–1883
Declarations of insolvency: country	B 6/176–177	1854–1869
Declarations of inability to pay debts	B 6/220–222	1897–1925
Certificates of Conformity	B 6/1–41	1833–1856

Registers of Commissioners of Bankrupts and Court of Bankruptcy, and fiats, 1710–1849, B 4/1-52 are incomplete until 1821 for London, and 1832 elsewhere, when the Court of Bankruptcy was established. Entries vary in detail over the period; included sometimes are the address and trade of the bankrupt (except 1770–1797), and the names of either the petitioning creditors or those of the bankrupt's agent or solicitor. A register entry underlined or ticked indicates a corresponding case file should be in Series B 3. Some registers have name indexes, but others simply have alphabetic sections in which the bankrupt was entered under the initial letter of their surname.

EXAMPLE: DOCKET REGISTER, 1839

	1839 Bankrupt	Description	Residence
28	Dredge John	Hotelkeeper	Liverpool
29	Dossen Henry	Currier	Bridgwater Somerset
30	Dadley John	Builder	Bedminster Bristol
31	Dalton William	Farmer	Skelton Yorkshire

Solicitor or Agent	Residence	Docket	Date of Fiat
Adlington Co	Bedford Row	27th July 1839	29th July 1839
Pain	New Inn	5th August	6th August 1839
Stevens	Grays Inn	6th August	10th August 1839
Baxters	Linc: Inn F^{ds}	12 August	13 August 1839

Bankruptcy

Registers of renewed Commissions of Bankruptcy, 1743–1833, are in Series B 4/53-56.

Series B 4 is searchable by date only on Discovery. These commissions and fiats, after 1758, may have been enrolled in B 5. There is an index to enrolments, 1825–1832, in B 8.

Petitions against Declarations of Bankruptcy, 1710–1877, B 1, give the background details recited prior to a decision being made. A Crown fee was paid before the estate was divided up. Other administrative records are in B 2, B 5–B 8 and B 11– B 12.

Docket Books record the commencement of proceedings containing information on the issue of commissions and renewed Commissions of Bankruptcy. From 1849, when the London Court of Bankruptcy was established, the series of London District and Country District General Docket Books in B 6 shows the class of certificate awarded or (after 1861) date of discharge, name, address and trade of the bankrupt and sometimes the names of petitioning creditors.

Creditors petitioned for Adjudication in Bankruptcy. There are two series of General Docket Books, 1849 to 1869: for the London District (B 6/99–117) and County District (B 6/118–124). There are also County Court Docket Books, 1861–1869 (B 6/125–132).

For London Court cases, 1861–1870, Deeds of Composition with creditors or of assignment to trustees are summarized in a series of registers in B 6 (indexes in B 8). Registers of Petitions for protection from bankruptcy process in County Court cases, from 1854, are in LCO 28.

There are indexed Registers of Certificates of Conformity for 1733 to 1817 and deposited Certificates, 1815 to 1856, B 6/1–41. From 1849 to 1861 there were three types of certificate: where the bankrupt was blameless; where some blame could be attributed; where it was entirely the bankrupt's fault. After 1861, Orders of Discharge were issued instead of Certificates of Conformity.

The Commissioners took statements from the bankrupt and his creditors about his debts and the creditors would then elect trustees or assignees to value his assets and distribute them as dividends. Full-time Official Assignees, to prevent fraud, were also appointed after 1831 and thereafter assignees had to pay cash from the sale of a bankrupt's estates into the Bank of England.

Enrolled copies of some Certificates of Conformity, 1710–1846; some assignments of assets to trustees, 1825–1834 and some appointments of trustees, 1832–1855, are in B 5. After 1861, Orders of Discharge were issued instead. Records relating to issues the Commissioners were unable to resolve or appeals in bankruptcy cases are in B 1 and B 7. Actions against individual bankrupts or their assignees may sometimes be found in the records of other courts – Chancery, Exchequer, King's Bench and Common Pleas – many cases coming before the Palace Court, which dealt with small debt cases in the Westminster area.

From 1861, insolvent debtors could apply for bankruptcy even if they were not traders. B 6/74-8 (1825–83), B 6/176-177 (1854–69) and B 6/220-222 (1897–1925) include declarations of insolvency and inability to pay. From 1825–54, these records cover London and county cases. After 1854, they cover London only. They usually show: date the declaration was filed; name, address and occupation of the debtor; debtor's solicitor's name.

Bankruptcy Proceedings from 1869

Petitions for Bankruptcy	B 6/184-197	1870–83
Creditors' petitions for bankruptcy adjudication	B 6/178-183	1870–83
Registers of petitions to the High Court	B 11	1884–1994
Registers of Receiving Orders	B 12	1887–1988
Registers of bankrupts in the London Courts	BT 40/25-33	1870 to 1886
Registers of bankrupts in the County Courts	BT 40/34-52	1870–84

Bankruptcy

Following the establishment of the London Court of Bankruptcy in 1869, there are: Registers of Petitions for Bankruptcy, 1870–1883, B 6/184-197 covering both town and country cases. They are arranged alphabetically by initial letter of the bankrupt's name, and give the name, occupation and address of the bankrupt person.

Registers of Creditors' Petitions for cases heard in London only, 1870 to 1883, are in B 6/178-183. They are arranged in date order and by bankrupt's surname and often include: name, address and occupation of the bankrupt and the petitioning creditor(s); details of what formal act of bankruptcy was committed (for example, filing a declaration on insolvency, or leaving the country); date (and place if outside London) of adjudication as a bankrupt; date of *London Gazette* advertisement; names of the trustees appointed; amount of dividend paid (as shillings in the pound); and date proceedings closed.

EXAMPLE: CREDITORS' PETITIONS FOR BANKRUPTCY ADJUDICATION
An example of an entry from B 6/178 relates to John Gunn:

Name of Bankrupt	Residence and Description	Trader
Gunn John 332	of N° 10 Austin Friars in the City of London Merchant trading in copartnership with William Jamieson at N° 10 Austin Friars aforesaid under the style or firm of Gunn Jamieson & C°	Trader

Indexes to Declarations of Inability to Pay (London Court cases only after 1854), which were one means of committing a formal act of bankruptcy, give the date of filing and basic details of the name, address and occupation of the debtor and name of his solicitor, 1825–1925, and are also in B 6.

From 1884 to 1994, there are Registers of Petitions to the High Court in B 11. The actual petitions will only survive if the Case File in B 9 survives.

Registers of Receiving Orders, 1887–1988, in B 12, contain dates of formal court orders, including: the order of discharge with a note of any conditions attached to it; and the date of the trustees' release.

Both B 11 and B 12 can be browsed by date on Discovery.

There are also Registers of Bankrupts in the London Courts, 1870 to 1886, BT 40/25-33 and County Courts, 1870-1884, BT 40/34-52.

The Minute Books of Lord Chancellor's records, 1714–1851, in B 7, record whether an order was issued. The records are very difficult to read but there is an index to the Series.

After 1883, the London Court of Bankruptcy was incorporated into the Supreme Court as the High Court of Justice in Bankruptcy. Petitions were only presented to the High Court if the debtor had resided or carried out business in the London District for six months, if he was not resident in England, or the creditor could not identify his place of residence. A High Court judge could transfer any case to or from a County Court. From 1883 Official Receivers, supervised by the Bankruptcy Department of the Board of Trade, administered a bankrupt's estate once a court had made a receiving order (see below).

Bankruptcy Appeals

Bankruptcy Appeals from 1864 to 1870 are in Series J 1, and from 1871–75 are in B 7 with entry books in B 1. Thereafter, appeals were directed to the Supreme Court's Court of Appeal and records are in J series: 1876–1955, J 15; from 1876, J 56; from 1918, J 69; from 1920, J 70.

From 1883, appeals in County Court case files went to a divisional court of the High Court: from 1864, J 60; from 1875, J 74; from 1920, J 95.

Both series are browsable by date on Discovery.

Bankruptcy

Bankruptcy Functions of the Board of Trade

Registers of Bankruptcies in London Bankruptcy Court	BT 40/25-33	1870–86
Registers of Bankruptcies in County Courts	BT 40/34-52	1870–84
Files of Dissolved Companies	BT 31	1855–1995
Search Registers and Indexes	BT 293	1884–1923
Estate Ledgers	BT 294	1884–about 1950
Deeds of Arrangement	BT 39	1888–1947
Deeds of Arrangement	BT 221	1897–1915
Case Files of the Official Receiver	BT 226	1891–1994

EXAMPLE: BOARD OF TRADE REGISTER FOR CHARLES LAVERCOMBE, 1902
G-O Index, 1899–1903 (BT 293/11):

| Name of Debtor | | Address and Description | Court | No | Year | Reference to Search Register |
Surname	Christian Names					
Lavercombe	Charles	Shepherds Bush Harness maker	High	828	1902	49-106
Laverick	George Colin	West Hartlepool, General Dealer	Sunderland	19	1899	40-4
Laverton	William	Aberavon Builder	Neath	13	1902	48-12
Laverton	William	St. Columb Cornwall Butcher	Truro	32	1899	40-5

Search Register Volume 49, 1902 (BT 293/73) provides a full address for Charles Lavercombe (177 Asken Road, Shepherds Bush) but little additional information other than dates of Orders, Filing etcetera.

From 1884, the Board of Trade supervised the official receivers, who acted as interim administrators of the bankrupt's assets, pending the appointment of a trustee. Registers of London court bankruptcies, 1870–86, are in BT 40/25-33 and County Court bankruptcies, 1870–84, in BT 40/34-52.

If the assets were less than £300, the receiver normally acted as trustee. Board of Trade registers in BT 293, covering the period 1884 to 1923, contain entries for all persons served with a petition for bankruptcy. They cover London and the counties. Not all petitions actually resulted in formal bankruptcy. There are further records in the BT series, including an incomplete series of Estate legers in BT 294, covering 1884 to about 1950, arranged by surname, which may show how the assets were distributed. Both BT 293 and BT 294 are browsable on Discovery by date and initial of the surname.

Proceedings leading to the liquidation and winding-up of companies may be found among the records of the Court of Bankruptcy. The files for dissolved companies registered in London from 1856, BT 31, usually consist of the following documents: the company's memorandum and articles of association and constitution; location of registered office and a register of directors; annual returns; liquidation and dissolution documents, including Return of Final Winding-up Meeting, and a copy of Court Order for compulsory winding-up. Notices of receiverships, liquidations and bankruptcies should be listed in the *London Gazette*. TNA's Research Guide *Registration of Companies and Business* gives more information.

Deeds of Arrangement, private agreements between debtor and creditors, became compulsory from 1888 and registers are in BT 39 from 1888 to 1947, with a small selection in BT 221 from 1897 to 1915. There is a selection of Deeds of Assignment covering various dates between 1899 and 1915. There are also some sample case papers in BT 221 covering dates from 1884 to the 1960s. Case files of the Official Receiver relating to High Court cases from 1891 are in BT 226, sampled from 1914. Pre-1914 cases are indexed by name in a card index available at TNA. Later indexes are in BT 293. Most cases are personal bankrupts, ranging from comedians to stockbrokers.

OSCAR WILDE
Oscar Fingel O'Flahertie Wills Wilde was one of many celebrities to have been declared bankrupt, along with Lionel Bart, George Best and Rembrandt.

Oscar Wilde, photo by Napoleon Sarony, 1882.

A writer and poet, Oscar Wilde (1854–1900) was forced to bankruptcy in 1895 following a trial in which he had sued John Sholts Douglas, the Marquess of Queensbury, for libel. Queensbury had accused him of committing the crime of sodomy. Queensbury was found not guilty and his acquittal meant that

Wilde, under the Libel Act 1843, was legally liable for the considerable expenses Queensbury had incurred in his defence. As a result, Wilde was forced into bankruptcy and many of his possessions were sold off, including the production rights to *The Importance of Being Ernest* and *Lady Windermere's Fan*.

The records held at The National Archives under Bankruptcy Proceedings (B 9/428-429) comprise two copious volumes. The first meeting of the creditors took place on 26 August 1895 when Oscar Wilde was described as 'late of 16 Tite Street, Chelsea, and now of Her Majesty's Prison, Wandsworth'. The Marquis had entered a claim for £670.13.8, the amount of the judgement, plus £6.10.0 costs. On 26 August 1895 Wilde was declared a bankrupt. Numerous other creditors followed suit, including: Alsop & Quiller, Dispensing Chemists for £36.10.0; The Savoy Hotel & Restaurant, for £63.7.10; The Hôtel Métropole, Brighton for £8.9.6; and Henry Simmons, Cigar Merchant of Piccadilly, for £23.5.9. Wilde's total debts were calculated as £3,591.0.0

Wilde died, intestate, on 30 November 1900 at the Hôtel d'Alsace, rue des Beaux Arts, Paris. Administration of his estate was granted on 22 February 1906, the Official Receiver becoming trustee of his estate. On 28 May 1906, Wilde's estate was declared solvent following payment of a final dividend giving creditors in bankruptcy 20s in the £, together with 4 percent interest.

In *The Picture of Dorian Grey*, Wilde had written:

> Many people become bankrupt through having invested too heavily in the prose of life. To have ruined one's self over poetry is an honour.

Chapter 11

NEWSPAPERS, PERIODICALS, JOURNALS AND DIRECTORIES

NEWSPAPERS, PERIODICALS AND JOURNALS
The *Gazettes*

The *Gazettes* are government publications, currently managed by the Stationery Office, under the superintendence of The National Archives. As the official public record, information published is verified and certified as fact. The first *Gazette* issued was in 1665, when King Charles II, having moved his court to Oxford to avoid the ravages of the plague in London, approved the first issue of a newspaper called the *Oxford Gazette*. When the court returned to London early the following year, the newspaper went with it and the first issue of the *London Gazette* was published on 5 February 1666. Although the nature of its contents has evolved over time, its standing as the official public record has remained.

Public notices regarding insolvent debtors and bankrupts, informing creditors about proceedings and applications for release, have appeared in the *London Gazette* for centuries. As part of the legal proceedings it was a formal requirement to alert creditors to forthcoming meetings concerning the bankrupt, while notices were also made when the debtor's bankruptcy was formally discharged, often many years later. Information in a bankruptcy notice may include the name of the bankrupt and his or her address, the names of any business partner(s), the court and appointed trustees through which the process was to be administered, the date of any forthcoming meetings, and requests for debts to the bankrupt to be paid and for creditors to submit claims.

Details of bankrupts appear from 1684; before 1832, they include many bankruptcies not included in the bankruptcy records at The National Archives. In 1712, the Act to Relieve Insolvent Debtors required that debtors' details were published in the *London Gazette*. Between 1813 and 1861 (and less frequently in earlier times) notices of the date and place of the hearing of petitions from insolvent debtors, usually but not always in prison, appear regularly. The *London Gazette* published notices of those who appeared before the Court for the Relief of Insolvent Debtors across the country, not just in the capital.

Complete copies of the *London Gazette* are held at the British Library, The National Archives and Guildhall Library. A very incomplete run, 1825–1962, is browsable on Ancestry.

Scottish notices would have been placed in the *Edinburgh Gazette*, first published in 1699, thirty-four years after the first edition of the *London Gazette*. It ran for forty-one issues, the last being on 17 July 1699. It reappeared sporadically but did not begin again as an unbroken and continuous publication run until 1793.

The *Belfast Gazette* was first published on 7 June 1921. Previously the same function was performed for the whole of Ireland by the *Dublin Gazette*, but with the partition of Ireland, a separate publication was required in Northern Ireland. The *Dublin Gazette* now continues in the Republic of Ireland as *Iris Oifigiúil*.

All historic issues of the three *Gazettes* are fully searchable online at **www.thegazette.co.uk**. The *Dublin Gazette*, which existed from 1706–1920, is not available on the website.

PERRY'S GAZETTE

It was from the notices published in the *Gazettes* that the lists published in *The Gentleman's Magazine*, *The Times* and other publications were derived. These included *Perry's Bankrupt & Insolvent Gazette* (1828–1861) – later *Perry's Bankrupt Weekly Gazette*

Newspapers, Periodicals, Journals and Directories

(1862–1881), then *Perry's Gazette* (1882–1964). This was a specialist bankruptcy and insolvency journal, founded in London in 1826 by Thomas Walter Perry (1780–1868). Perry's original Bankrupt and Insolvency Registry Office for protection against frauds, swindlers etc., was established in London in 1810. Earlier issues include the name of the bankrupt, the date gazetted, and their address and trade. Additional information can include whether the proceedings were taking place due to the bankrupt's own petition, or at the demand of petitioning creditors, whose names, trades and addresses are also given. In later editions the bankrupt is often merely referred to by name and trade.

Perry's also included 'Irish bankrupts and Scottish Sequestrations' and lists of dissolutions of partnerships gazetted in England and Wales. The British Newspaper Archive **www.british newspaperarchive.co.uk** has the following titles in or planned for its digital archive: 1828–1861 *Perry's Bankrupt and Insolvent Gazette*; and 1862–1871 *Perry's Bankrupt Weekly Gazette*. The 1891 edition of *Perry's Gazette* is available on TheGenealogist.

THE GENTLEMAN'S MAGAZINE

The Gentleman's Magazine, or *The Gentleman's Magazine and Monthly Intelligencer* as it was originally titled, was first published in January 1731. In 1736 it became *The Gentleman's Magazine and Historical Chronicle*, and from 1834 *The Gentleman's Magazine*. It finally ceased publication in 1922. Published monthly, *The Gentleman's Magazine* covered a vast range of topics, from share prices to poetry. From its inception to 1868 it included items such as court proceedings, inheritances and bankrupts, mostly gleaned from the *London Gazette*, as well as local and national newspapers. Intriguingly, the lists of bankrupts are usually headed B–NK–TS, or similar. 'Bankrupts' was used from 1740s–1780s.

The National Archives and the British Library have complete runs to 1868. Many other libraries around the country also have sets, but many of these are incomplete. Additionally, the Internet Archive www.archive.org has many volumes collected from several libraries.

Each volume had its own internal index under a number of separate headings. For the family historian the name indexes are the most important. Unfortunately, until the nineteenth century no forenames or initials are given. There are a number of other indexes that have been produced over the years. These include the two-volume *A general index to the first fifty-six volumes of The Gentleman's Magazine...* (1731–1786), which was compiled by Samuel Ayscough in 1789. Volumes 3 and 4 were published in 1821 as *A general index to the Gentleman's Magazine ... 1787–1818*. There are several published and manuscript indexes to births, marriages and obituaries covering various periods. The historic indexes have to all intents and purposes been superseded by the availability of fully searchable digitized versions available online. The most complete index is *The Gentleman's Magazine Index*, compiled in seventy-five volumes by the College of Arms. This has been microfilmed by FamilySearch; an incomplete set is available at the Society of Genealogists.

The Bodleian Internet Library of Early Journals, a digital library of eighteenth and nineteenth-century journals, **www.bodley.ox.ac.uk/ilej/journals** has page images for volumes 1–20, 1731–50.

The Hathi Trust has all volumes except 1731–77, 1779–1907, scanned from the University of Michigan and the New York Public Library (**http://catalog.hathitrust.org/Record/000542092**). It also has all volumes from 1736 to 1849, scanned from Indiana and Harvard Universities (**http://catalog.hathitrust.org/Record/0060566**). Because of the inconsistency in volume numbering and multiple series, looking up volumes by date is more effective than by number.

The Gentleman's Magazine, vol.56. (1786)

The London Magazine or *Gentleman's Monthly Intelligencer*
The London Magazine, the oldest literary periodical, was founded in 1732 and ran for fifty-three years until its closure in 1785. In 1820, the *London Magazine* was resurrected, but again ceased publication in 1829. The journal regularly published lists of 'Persons declared Bankrupts'. The Hathi Trust (see above) has copies of the first series, 1732–85.

List of persons declared bankrupts, published in The London Magazine or Gentleman's Monthly Intelligencer, *October 1732.*

THE JURIST
The Jurist was published by Henry Sweet from January 1837 to January 1855. Included were details of both bankrupts and insolvent debtors, taken from the *London Gazette*. The Hathi Trust (see above) has copies of the complete run.

THE EUROPEAN MAGAZINE & LONDON REVIEW
Similarly, *The European Magazine & London Review*, published twice-yearly 1782–1826, also provided its readers with lists of bankruptcies.

> FRIDAY, March 31.
> BANKRUPTS.
> ALFRED OCTAVIUS TANNER, Edmonton, Middlesex, fruiterer, dealer and chapman, April 7 at half-past 1, and May 12 at half-past 11, Court of Bankruptcy, London: Off. Ass. Cannan; Sol. Towne, 9, Devonshire-square, Bishopsgate.—Fiat dated March 11.
> WILLIAM BEACH, Salisbury, Wiltshire, cutler and surgical instrument maker, April 13 at half-past 1, and May 12 at half-past 12, Court of Bankruptcy, London: Off. Ass. Cannan; Sol. Jones, Quality-court, London.—Fiat dated March 30.
> JOHN BATES, Kettering, Northamptonshire, watch maker and auctioneer, April 13 and May 12 at 1, Court of Bankruptcy, London: Off. Ass. Whitmore; Sol. Fearnhead, 17, Clifford's-inn, London.—Fiat dated March 30.
> JAMES GREEN, Barbican, London, wholesale hat and cap warehouseman and cap manufacturer, leather seller, shoe factor, and general agent, dealer and chapman, April 7 at 2, and May 12 at 12, Court of Bankruptcy, London: Off. Ass. Pennell; Sol. Depree, 9, Lawrence-lane, Cheapside.—Fiat dated March 30.
> GEORGE DUGLAS, Brunswick-place, Old Kent-road, Surrey, linen draper, dealer and chapman, April 11 at half-past 1, and May 12 at 11, Court of Bankruptcy, London: Off. Ass. Stansfeld; Sol. Cooper, 17, Hatton-garden.—Fiat dated March 28.
> DANIEL GREENAWAY PORTER, Great Tower-street, London, wine merchant, April 7 and May 18 at 12, Court of Bankruptcy, London: Off. Ass. Follett; Sols. Tilson & Co., Coleman-street.—Fiat dated March 18.
> JOHN ROBERTS and WILLIAM HAMMILL ROBERTS, Liverpool, ironmongers and ship smiths, dealers and chapmen, (carrying on trade under the firm of John Roberts & Son), April 19 and May 5 at 11, District Court of Bankruptcy, Liverpool: Off. Ass. Turner; Sols. Grocott, Liverpool; Johnson & Co., Temple, London.—Fiat dated March 25.

The Jurist, *No.586, Vol.XII*, 1 April 1848.

'A List of Bankrupts from December 24, 1811, to June 19, 1812', published in The European Magazine & London Review, *Vol.61* (January–June 1812).

A.

ABSOLON, G. Wallingford, innkeeper, Dec. 31. [Vandercom and Co. Bush-lane.]
Anderson, D. Billiter-lane, merchant, Jan. 4. [Wilde and Co. Castle-street, Falcon-square.]
Ashfield, T. Shadwell, money-scrivener, Jan. 7. [Nelson, Palsgrave-place.]
Adlington, E. A. Liverpool, tobacconist, Jan. 18. [Parr and Co. Liverpool.]
Anderson, J. Newcastle-upon-Tyne, flax dresser, Jan. 28. [Bell and Co. Bow-lane.]
Atkinson, W. Liverpool, liquor merchant, Jan. 28. [Blackstock and Co. Temple.]
Aldridge, J. Maidenhead, corn chandler, Feb. 1. [Benbow, Lincoln's-inn.] Superseded May 2.
Ancell, J. Rushey-mead, Wallington, Surrey, calico printer, Feb. 1. [Annesley and Co. Tokenhouse-yard.]
Ashley, J. and T. Primrose-street, Bishopsgate, silk weavers, Feb. 4. [Collins and Co. Spital-square.]
Anderson, W. Bolton, druggist, Feb. 8. [Windle, John-street, Bedford-row.]
Ansell, T. Birmingham, baker, Feb. 8. [Smart, Staple-inn.]
Arden, J. Blackmore-street, Clare-market, grocer, Feb. 15. [Swann, New Basinghall-street.]
Abbotts, G. Laches, Staffordshire, corn dealer, Feb, 15. [Willis and Co. Warnford-court.]
Adkin, L. Ainsworth, Lancashire, dealer, Feb. 29.

Andrews, T. Brewham Lodge, Somersetshire, farmer, May 12. [Holmes and Co. Clement's-inn.]
Aldridge, J. Reading, grocer, June 2. [Eyre, Gray's-inn.]
Ackrill, R. jun. Worcester, shopkeeper, June 6. [Wall, Worcester.]
Aaron, A. Spark's-court, Duke's-place, spectacle maker, June 13. [Harris, Castle-street, Houndsditch.]
Ashbie, T. Monckton Farley, quarryman, June 16. [Baxter and Co. Furnival's-inn.]

B.

Buckley, G. Tame Water, Yorkshire, manufacturer, Dec. 24. [Milne and Co. Temple.]
Bilger, M. sen. and M. jun. Piccadilly, goldsmiths and jewellers, Dec. 24. [Aldridge and Co. Lincoln's-inn.]
Brown, T. Liverpool, merchant, Dec. 28. [Cooper and Co. Southampton-buildings.]
Barker, R. Kingston-upon-Hull, merchant, Dec. 31. [Rosser and Son, Bartlett's-buildings.]
Boldero, C. Boldero, E. G. Lushington, Sir H. and Boldero, H. Cornhill, bankers, Jan. 4. [Lamb, Prince's-street, Bank.]
Barnacott, T. Plymouth, carpenter, Jan. 14. [Drewe and Co. New-inn.]
Butler, C. Old Jewry, broker, Jan. 14. [Batchellor

Provincial Newspapers

Reports in local or national newspapers can often be the first indication of a debtor or bankrupt ancestor, which can lead to any surviving official records. Provincial newspapers were published in many parts of the country from the early eighteenth century. However, until the mid-nineteenth century, these usually relied on national or international news for their content. However, they also could include details of bankrupts and insolvent debtors.

Local newspapers are, as is to be expected, held locally, in libraries, local studies libraries and so on. The national collection is held by the British Library, mostly out-housed at Boston Spa near Wetherby in Yorkshire and requiring 48 hours to arrive at the British Library Newsroom. There is also a public reading room at Boston Spa itself.

The British Library collection of British newspapers is fairly comprehensive from the 1840s onwards. Since 1869, British and Irish newspapers have been received through legal deposit, by which publishers are required to send one copy of each issue to the British Library. The collection therefore includes full runs of the main London edition of all the British national daily and Sunday newspapers. Most daily and weekly provincial newspapers are also held, including some from the early eighteenth century onwards. The British Library's newspaper catalogue can be found at **http://explore.bl.uk**, selecting the main catalogue's advanced option and 'Newspapers' from the list of materials.

The Commiſſioners in a renew'd Commiſſion of Bankrupt againſt Thomas Hopper, late of the City of Briſtol, Hoſier, deceaſed, intend to meet on Thurſday the 17th of December next, at Ten in the Forenoon, at the Houſe of Mary Leadbeater, Widow, in All Saints Lane in Briſtol, commonly call'd the Elephant Coffee-Houſe; in order to make a 3d Dividend of the ſaid Bankrupt's Eſtate.

Stamford Mercury, *28 November 1717.*

The British Library also holds the Burney Collection of seventeenth and eighteenth-century newspapers, which has been digitized. Also, the Nineteenth-Century Newspapers Digital Archive, a full run of forty-eight British newspapers 1800 to 1900. Both can be searched for free on site at the British Library.

There are several UK newspaper websites. The broadest general collection of newspapers available online is provided by the British Newspaper Archive through its subscription website **www.british newspaperarchive.co.uk**. This is a partnership between the British Library and Findmypast to digitize up to 40 million newspaper pages from the British Library's vast collection and grows week on week as additional pages are added. A version is also available on Findmypast.

Several English and Irish newspapers are also available on the subscription website **www.newspapers.com**. Access is also available with an Ancestry 'All Access Membership' subscription.

Other websites offering access to digitized copies of local newspapers include:

Last Chance to Read: **www.lastchancetoread.com**
The Scotsman Digital Archive: **http://archive.scotsman.com**
Welsh Newspapers Online: **http://newspapers.library.wales**

The NEWSPLAN databases can help locate copies of local newspapers across Britain. The collaborative initiative began in the late 1980s to help preserve and collate holdings **www.bl.uk/ reshelp/bldept/news/newsplan/newsplan.html**.

NEWSPLAN is based on ten regions, corresponding to the ten regional library systems, for which there are currently listings for Ireland, London and South Eastern Region, Scotland, South West Region (Devon Newspaper bibliography only) and Wales/Cymru.

An extensive list of links to newspaper databases from around the world is at **https://en.wikipedia.org/wiki/Wikipedia:List_of_ online_newspaper_archives**. This includes many titles from the United Kingdom.

DIRECTORIES

Many London and county directories published lists of bankrupts. For example, *The City of London Directory* was first published in 1871 and included details of 'Bankruptcies and Liquidations' during the year.

There is also *The bankrupt directory, being a complete register of all the bankrupts, with their residences, trades & dates when they appeared in the London Gazette, from December 1820 to April 1843*; compiled by George Elwick, published by Simpkin, Marshall & Co. (1843). The volume includes about 29,000 names, arranged alphabetically, with place, occupation and date of publication in the *London Gazette*. The entries have been transcribed on Findmypast. For example, the volume includes the brief entry:

> Burgess Richard and John, Macclesfield, silk throwsters, May 7, 1841.

Bankruptcies & Liquidations, listed in The City of London Directory, *1877.*

However, this does enable the entry in the *London Gazette* to be discovered relatively easily, where the full entry reads:

> Whereas a Fiat in Bankruptcy is awarded and issued forth against Richard Burgess and John Burgess, of Macclesfield, in the county palatine of Chester, Silk Thrower, Dealers, Chapmen, and Copartners, and they being declared bankrupts are hereby required to surrender themselves to Joshua Evans,

Esq. one of His Majesty's Commissioners of the Court of Bankruptcy, in Basinhall-street, in the city of London, and make a full discovery and disclosure of their estate and effects; when and where the creditors are to come prepared to prove their debts, and at the first sitting to choose assignees, and at the last sitting the said bankrupts are to assent or dissent from the allowance of their certificate. All persons indebted to the said bankrupts, or that have any of their effect, are not to pay or deliver the same, but to Mr. Patrick Johnson, the Official Assignee, whom the Commissioner has appointed, and give notice to Messrs. Crowder and Maynard, Solicitors, Mansion-house-place, London.

Bankrupts in England, Scotland and Wales in the year 1851, compiled by M. Shaw-Guisset (2000), contains information on more than 3,000 bankruptcy petitions filed in England and Wales in 1851. These were extracted from *The Jurist* and include name, address, occupation and date.

A further volume, *Bankrupts in England and Wales in the year 1861*, by the same compiler (2001), contains information on more than 3,000 bankruptcy petitions filed in England and Wales in 1861. These too were extracted from *The Jurist* and provide the same information.

Other similar works include:

An alphabetical list of all the bankrupts from the first of January, 1774 to the thirtieth of June, 1786, inclusive, with the date of the certificates & supersedures, to those who have received them (1786).

Bailey's list of bankrupts, dividends and certificates from the year 1772 to 1793, both included, with names and residence of the different solicitors under each (1784)

William Smith's *A List of bankrupts, with their dividends, certificates, &c. &c. for the last twenty years and six months, viz. from Jan. 1, 1786, to June 24, 1806, inclusive ... ; and A list of bankrupts, with their dividends, certificates ... from July 1806, to Jan. 1, 1808, : being a continuation of the last twenty years and six months, viz. from Jan. 1, 1786, to June 24, 1806* ... (1806 and 1808). This is also available on TheGenealogist.

The annual *The Bankrupts' Register* for the years 1832–47 (1833–48).

Appendix A

ACTS OF PARLIAMENT

Acts of Parliament concerning debtors, imprisonment sanctuary and bankruptcy in England, in chronological order to 1901.

1275	3 Edward I c. 23	Distress for Debt Against Strangers Act
1285	13 Edward I	Recovery of Debts by Statute Merchant Act
1285	13 Edward I c. 19	Intestates' Debts Act
1351	25 Edward III c. 12	Crown Debtors Act
1377	1 Richard II c. 12	Prisoners for Debt Act
1382	6 Richard II c. 2	Venue in Actions for Debt, etc. Act
1530	22 Henry VIII c. 3	Plumstead Marsh (Existing Debts) Act
1531	25 Henry VIII c. 6	Recognizances for Debt Act
1535	27 Henry VIII c. 19	Sanctuary Act
1542	34 & 35 Henry VIII c. 4	Statute of Bankrupts
1571	13 Elizabeth I c. 7	Bankrupts Act
1603	1 James I c. 14	(Small debts, etc., London)
1603	1 James I c. 15	(Bankrupts)
1604	2 James I c.25	Repeal of Sanctuary Laws
1605	3 James I c. 15	(Small debts, London City)
1623	21 James I c. 19	(Bankrupts)
1623	21 James 1 c. 28	(Continuance of Acts, etc.)
1690	2 William & Mary Sess. 2 c. 15	Insolvent Debtors Relief Act

Appendix A

Year	Citation	Act
1694	5 & 6 William & Mary c. 8	Insolvent Debtors Relief Act
1695	7 & 8 William 3 c.35.	Marriage Duty Act
1695	7 & 8 William III c. 12	Insolvent Debtors Relief Act
1696	8 & 9 William III c. 18	Compositions by Debtors Act
1696	8 & 9 c. 27 William III	Escape of Debtors, etc. Act
1697	William III c. 299	Composition by Debtors Act
1701	1 Ann stat. 1 c. 25	An Act for the Relief of poor Prisoners for Debt.
1701	1 Ann stat. 2 c. 6	An act for the better preventing escapes out of the Queen's Bench and Fleet Prisons.
1704	2 & 3 Ann c. 16	An Act for the Discharge of Insolvent Debtors
1705	4 Ann c. 17:	Bankrupts Act
1705	6 Ann c. 22	Bankrupts Act
1706	6 Ann c. 9	Escape from prisons Act
1711	10 Ann c. 15	Customs and Excise Act
1711	10 Ann. c. 29	Insolvent Debtors' Relief Act
1711	10 Ann. c. 25	Bankrupts Act
1716	George I c. 123	Bankruptcy Act
1718	George I c. 245	Bankrupts Act
1719	George I c. 226	Insolvent Debtors' Relief, etc. Act
1720	7 George I stat.1 c. 31	Bankrupts Act
1722	9 George I c. 22	Criminal Law Act (the so-called "Black Act")
1722	9 George I c. 28	The Mint in Southwark Act
1724	11 George I c. 21	Insolvent Debtors Relief Act

1724	11 George I c. 22	Shelterers in Wapping, Stepney, etc. Act
1725	12 George I c. 29	Frivolous Arrests Act
1728	2 George II c. 20	Insolvent Debtors Relief Act
1728	2 George II c. 22	Insolvent Debtors Relief Act
1729	2 Geo II c.20	An Act for the Relief of Insolvent Debtors
1729	3 George II c. 27	Insolvent Debtors Relief Act
1731	5 George II c. 27	Process for Small Debts Act
1731	5 George II c. 30	Bankrupts Act
1736	10 George II c. 26	Insolvent Debtors Relief Act
1737	11 George II c. 9	Insolvent Debtors Relief Act
1740	14 George II c. 10	Small Debts, London Act
1740	14 George II c. 34	Continuance of Acts, 1740 c. 34
1742	16 George II c. 17	Insolvent Debtors Relief Act
1742	16 George II c. 27	Bankrupts Act
1745	19 George II c. 32	Bankrupts Act
1747	21 George II c. 3	Vexatious Arrests Act
1747	21 George II c. 31	Insolvent Debtors Relief Act
1747	21 George II c. 33	Insolvent Debtors Relief, etc. Act
1748	22 George II c. 47	Small Debts, Southwark, etc. Act
1749	23 George II c. 33	Small Debts, Middlesex Act
1749	23 George II c. 30	Small Debts, Tower Hamlets Act
1749	23 George II c. 27	Small Debts, Westminster Act
1750	24 George II c. 16	Small Debts, Lincoln Act
1750	24 George II c. 42	Small Debts, Westminster Act
1751	25 George II c. 34	Small Debts, Birmingham Act
1751	25 George II c. 45	Small Debts, Canterbury Act
1751	George II 25 c. 43	Small Debts, Liverpool Act
1751	25 George II c. 38	Small Debts, Saint Albans Act
1753	26 George II c. 57	Debtors' Prison, Devonshire. Act
1753	26 George II c. 7	Small Debts, Boston Act
1753	26 George II c. 33	Clandestine Marriages Act
1755	28 George II c. 13	Insolvent Debtors Relief Act

Appendix A

1756	29 George II c. 18	Insolvent Debtors Relief Act
1756	29 George II c. 19	Juries Act
1757	31 George II c. 23	Brixton: Small Debts Act
1757	31 George II c. 24	Yarmouth: Small Debts Act
1758	32 George II c. 28	Debtors Imprisonment Act
1758	32 George II c. 6	Small Debts, Southwark, etc. Act
1760	1 George III c. 17	Insolvent Debtors Relief Act
1761	2 George III c. 2	Insolvent Debtors Relief Act
1762	2 George III c. 38	Kingston-upon-Hull: Small Debts Act
1761	2 George III c. 2	Insolvent Debtors Relief Act
1763	3 George III c. 19	Small Debts, Wiltshire Act
1763	4 George III c. 33	Bankrupts Act
1763	4 George III c. 36	Bankrupts, etc. Act
1763	4 George III c. 40	Doncaster: Small Debts, Lighting, etc. Act
1764	4 George III c. 41	Kirby, Westmorland: Small Debts Act
1765	5 George III c. 8	Small Debts, Blackheath, etc. Act
1765	5 George III c. 9	Small Debts, Chippenham Act
1765	5 George III c. 41	Insolvent Debtors Relief Act
1766	6 George III c. 6	Small Debts, Kent, etc. Act
1766	6 George III c. 16	Small Debts, Bath Act
1766	6 George III c. 20	Small Debts, Derby Act
1769	9 George III c. 26	Insolvent Debtors Relief Act
1770	10 George III c. 20	King's Lynn: Small Debts Act
1770	10 George III c. 21	Lancashire: Small Debts Act
1770	10 George III c. 29	Blackheath, etc., Small Debts Act
1772	13 George III c. 23	Relief of Insolvent Debtors, etc. Act
1772	13 George III c. 27	Exeter: Small Debts Act
1772	12 George III c. 47	Bankrupts Act
1772	12 George III c. 58	Gaols Act
1772	12 George III c. 66	Kidderminster: Small Debts Act
1774	14 George III c. 59	Health of Prisons Act
1774	14 George III c. 77	Insolvent Debtors, etc., Relief Act

1775	15 George III c. 64	Elloe, Lincoln: Small Debts Act
1776	17 George III c. 15	Yorkshire: Small Debts Act
1776	17 George III c. 19	Old Swineford: Small Debts Act
1776	16 George III c. 38	Insolvent Debtors Relief Act
1777	17 George III c. 62	Lincolnshire: Small Debts Act
1778	18 George III c. 34	Lincolnshire: Small Debts Act
1778	18 George III c. 36	Isle of Ely: Small Debts Act
1778	18 George III c. 43	Lincoln: Small Debts Act
1778	18 George III c. 52	Insolvent Debtors Relief, etc. Act
1779	19 George III c. 43	Lincolnshire: Small Debts Act
1779	19 George III c. 68	Small Debts, Tower Hamlets Act
1780	20 George III c. 64	Release of Prisoners by Rioters Act
1780	20 George III c. 65	West Riding: Small Debts Act
1781	21 George III c .1	Destruction of Prisons by Rioters Act
1781	21 George III c. 38	Small Debts, Beverley Act
1781	21 George III c. 63	Insolvent Debtors Relief Act
1782	22 George III c. 27	Small Debts, Kent Act
1783	23 George III c. 73	Shrewsbury: Small Debts Act
1783	24 George III Sess. 1 c. 8	Kent: Small Debts Act
1785	25 George III c. 7	Small Debts, Kent Act
1785	25 George III c. 45	Debtors, Middlesex Act
1786	26 George III c. 18	Kent: Small Debts Act
1786	26 George III c. 22	Kent: Small Debts Act
1786	26 George III c. 38	Imprisonment of Debtors, etc. Act
1786	26 George III c. 44	Relief and Debtors Act
1786	26 George III c. 118	Kent: Small Debts Act
1792	32 George III c. 77	Gloucestershire: Small Debts Act
1793	33 George III c. 5	Debtors Relief Act
1793	33 George III c. 84	West Riding: Small Debts Act
1794	34 George III c. 57	Bankrupts Act
1794	34 George III c. 69	Insolvent Debtors' Discharge Act
1795	35 George III c. 88	Insolvent Debtor's Discharge Act
1797	37 George III c. 112	Relief of Insolvent Debtors Act

Appendix A

1797	37 George III c. 124	Bankrupts Act
1799	39 George III c. 50	Relief of Debtors Act
1801	41 George III c. 64	Debtors Relief Act
1801	41 George III c. 70	Insolvent Debtors Relief Act
1804	44 George III c. 108	Insolvent Debtors Relief Act
1805	45 George III c. 3	Insolvent Debtors Relief Act
1806	46 George III c. 108	Insolvent Debtors Relief Act
1806	46 George III c. 135	Bankrupts Act
1808	48 George III c. 123	Discharge of Certain Imprisoned Debtors Act
1809	49 George II c. 6	Relief of Prisoners for Debt Act
1809	49 George III c. 115	Insolvent Debtors Relief Act
1809	49 George II c. 121	Bankrupts (England and Ireland) Act
1811	51 George III c. 125	Insolvent Debtors Relief (England) Act
1812	52 George III c. 13	Insolvent Debtors Relief (England) Act
1812	52 George III c. 34	Debtors Relief Act
1812	52 George III c. 160	Relief of Debtors in Prison Act
1812	52 George III c. 165	Insolvent Debtors Relief (England) Act
1812	53 George III c. 6	Insolvent Debtors Relief (England) Act
1813	53 George III c. 102	Insolvent Debtors (England) Act
1813	53 George III c. 21	Prisoners for Certain Debts, etc. Act
1813	54 George III c. 23	Insolvent Debtors (England) Act
1813	54 George III c. 28	Insolvent Debtors Relief (England) Act
1815	55 George III c. 50	Goal Fees Abolition Act
1816	56 George III c. 102	Insolvent Debtors (England) Act
1816	56 George III c. 137	Bankrupts (England) Act
1819	59 George III c. 129	Insolvent Debtors (England) Act
1820	1 George IV c. 3	Insolvent Debtors (England) Act
1820	1 George IV c. 119	Insolvent Debtors (England) Act
1821	1 & 2 George IV c. 59	Insolvent Debtors (Ireland) Act
1821	1 & 2 George IV c. 115	Bankruptcy Court Act
1822	3 George IV c. 74	Bankrupts Act

1822	3 George IV c. 81	Bankrupt Laws (England) Act
1822	3 George IV c. 123	Insolvent Debtors (England) Act
1823	4 George IV c. 64	Gaols etc. (England) Act
1824	5 George IV c. 61	Insolvent Debtors (England) Act
1824	5 George IV c. 98	Bankruptcy (England) Act
1825	6 George IV c. 16	Bankrupts (England) Act
1825	6 George IV c. 121	Insolvent Debtors Act
1826	7 George IV c. 57	Insolvent Debtors (England) Act
1827	7 & 8 George IV c. 71	Imprisonment for Debt Act
1830	11 George IV & I William IV c. 38	Insolvent Debtors (England) Act
1831	1 & 2 William IV c. 56	Bankruptcy Court (England) Act
1832	2 & 3 William IV c. 43	Insolvent Debtors Act
1832	2 & 3 William IV c. 44	Insolvent Debtors Act
1833	3 & 4 William IV c. 47	Court of Bankruptcy (England) Act
1835	5 & 6 William IV c. 29	Bankruptcy Act
1835	5 & 6 William IV c. 38	Prisons Act
1836	6 & 7 William IV c. 27	Bankruptcy Act
1836	6 & 7 William IV c. 44	Insolvent Debtors (England) Act
1839	2 & 3 Victoria c. 29	Bankruptcy Act
1839	2 & 3 Victoria c. 39	Insolvent Debtors Act
1839	2 & 3 Victoria c. 60	Debts Recovery Act
1842	5 & 6 Victoria c. 83	St. Briavels Small Debts Court Act
1842	5 & 6 Victoria c. 98	Prisons Act
1842	5 & 6 Victoria c. 116	Insolvent Debtors Act

Appendix A

1842	5 & 6 Victoria c. 122	Bankruptcy Act
1844	7 & 8 Victoria c. 70	Arrangements Between Debtors and Creditors Act
1845	8 & 9 Victoria c. 48	Bankruptcy Act
1845	8 & 9 Victoria c. 127	Small Debts Act
1846	9 & 10 Victoria c. 10	Small Debts Recovery Act
1847	10 & 11 Victoria c. 102	Bankruptcy, etc. Act
1848	11 & 12 Victoria c. 77	Insolvent Debtors, Court Act
1848	11 & 12 Victoria c. 86	Bankrupts Release Act
1848	11 & 12 Victoria c. 87	Debts Recovery Act
1849	12 & 13 Victoria c. 101	County Courts Act
1849	12 & 13 Victoria c. 106	Bankruptcy Law Consolidation Act
1850	13 & 14 Victoria c. 61	County Courts Act
1851	14 & 15 Victoria c. 52	Absconding Debtors Arrest Act
1852	15 & 16 Victoria c. 77	Bankruptcy Act
1853	16 & 17 Victoria c. 81	Bankruptcy Court Act
1854	17 & 18 Victoria c. 119	Bankruptcy Act
1857	20 & 21 Victoria c. 60	Bankrupt and Insolvent Act
1860	23 & 24 Victoria c. 147	Debtors and Creditors Act
1861	24 & 25 Victoria c. 134	Bankruptcy Act
1862	25 & 26 Victoria c. 99	Bankruptcy Act (1861) Amendment Act
1862	25 & 26 Victoria c. 104	Queen's Prison Discontinuance Act
1868	31 & 32 Victoria c. 104	Bankruptcy Amendment Act
1869	32 & 33 Victoria c. 62	Debtors Act
1869	32 & 33 Victoria c. 71	Bankruptcy Act
1869	32 & 33 Victoria c. 83	Bankruptcy Repeal and Insolvent Court Act
1870	33 & 34 Victoria c. 76	Absconding Debtors Act
1871	34 & 35 Victoria c. 50	Bankruptcy Disqualification Act
1873	36 & 37 Victoria c. 66	Supreme Court of Judicature Act
1875	38 & 39 Victoria c. 77	Supreme Court of Judicature Act
1878	41 & 42 Victoria c. 54	Debtors Act

1883	46 & 47 Victoria c. 52	Bankruptcy Act
1884	47 & 48 Victoria c. 9	Bankruptcy Appeals (County Courts) Act
1885	48 & 49 Victoria c. 47	Bankruptcy (Office Accommodation) Act
1886	49 & 50 Victoria c. 12	Bankruptcy (Office Accommodation) Act
1886	49 & 50 Victoria c. 28	Bankruptcy (Agricultural Labourers' Wages) Act
1887	50 & 51 Victoria c. 66	Bankruptcy (Discharge and Closure) Act
1888	51 & 52 Victoria c. 62	Preferential Payments in Bankruptcy Act
1890	53 & 54 Victoria c. 71	Bankruptcy Act
1897	60 & 61 Victoria c. 19	Preferential Payments in Bankruptcy Amendment Act

Appendix B

REGNAL YEARS

Monarch	Regnal year begin date	End of final year
William I	14 October 1066	9 September 1087
William II	26 September 1087	2 August 1100
Henry I	5 August 1100	1 December 1135
Stephen	26 December 1135	25 October 1154
Henry II	19 December 1154	6 July 1189
Richard I	3 September 1189	6 April 1199
John [see note 1]	27 May 1199	19 October 1216
Henry III	28 October 1216	16 November 1272
Edward I	20 November 1272	7 July 1307
Edward II	8 July 1307	20 January 1326/27
Edward III	25 January 1326/27	21 June 1377
Richard II	22 June 1377	29 September 1399
Henry IV	30 September 1399	20 March 1412/13
Henry V	21 March 1412/13	31 August 1422
Henry VI	1 September 1422	4 March 1460/61
Edward IV	4 March 1460/61	9 April 1483
Edward V	9 April 1483	25 June 1483
Richard III	26 June 1483	22 August 1485
Henry VII	22 August 1485	21 April 1509
Henry VIII	22 April 1509	28 January 1546/47
Edward VI	28 January 1546/47	6 July 1553
Jane [see note 2]	6 July 1553	17 July 1553
Mary I	6 July 1553	24 July 1554
Philip and Mary	25 July 1554	17 November 1558

Elizabeth I	17 November 1558	24 March 1602/03
James I	25 March 1603	27 March 1625
Charles I	27 March 1625	30 January 1648/49
Charles II [see note 3]	30 January 1648/49	6 February 1684/85
James II	6 February 1684/85	11 December 1688
William and Mary	13 February 1687/88	27 December 1694
William III	28 December 1694	8 March 1701/02
Anne	8 March 1701/02	1 August 1714
George I	1 August 1714	11 June 1727
George II	11 June 1727	25 October 1760
George III	25 October 1760	29 January 1820
George IV	29 January 1820	26 June 1830
William IV	26 June 1830	20 June 1837
Victoria	20 June 1837	22 January 1901
Edward VII	22 January 1901	6 May 1910
George V	6 May 1910	20 January 1936
Edward VIII	20 January 1936	11 December 1936
George VI	11 December 1936	5 February 1952
Elizabeth II	6 February 1952	

[1] John of England's regnal years are unusual for not starting on the same date every year, but rather on Ascension Day, a movable feast of the liturgical calendar.

[2] Lady Jane Grey, who was Queen Jane from 6 July 1553 to 17 July 1553, is not present in the official record. Mary I's reign officially begins on 6 July 1553.

[3] The Commonwealth era (1649–1660) is obliterated from the official record. The beginning regnal date of Charles II is 30 January 1649, the day his father was executed. However, Charles II would only become *de facto* king on 29 May 1660, officially regarded as the twelfth year of his reign. During the Commonwealth, public documents did not have any regnal or republican calendar, just the conventional calendar date, the 'The Year of Our Lord', with normal month and day.

USEFUL ADDRESSES AND WEBSITES

The National Archives
Kew
Richmond
Surrey TW9 4DU
telephone: 020 8876 3444
email via website
website: www.nationalarchives.gov.uk/

London Metropolitan Archives
40 Northampton Road
London EC1R 0HB
telephone: 020 7332 3820
email: ask.lma@cityoflondon.gov.uk
website: www.cityoflondon.gov.uk/things-to-do/london-metropolitan-archives/Pages/default.aspx

Society of Genealogists
14 Charterhouse Buildings
Goswell Road
London EC1M 7BA
telephone: 020 7251 8799
email: library@sog.org.uk
website: www.sog.org.uk/

Surrey History Centre
130 Goldsworth Road
Woking
Surrey GU21 6ND
telephone: 01483 518 737
email: shs@surreycc.gov.uk
website: www.surreycc.gov.uk/heritage-culture-and-recreation/archives-and-history/surrey-history-centre

AIM25
Archives in London and the M25 area.
www.aim25.com

Alsatia
History, context and meanings of London's sanctuaries other similar 'outlaw' areas
http://alsatia.org.uk/site/

British History Online
Digital library of key printed primary and secondary sources for the history of Britain and Ireland, with a primary focus on the period between 1300 and 1800.
www.british-history.ac.uk/

Find an Archive
Contact details for record repositories in the United Kingdom and also for institutions elsewhere in the world.
http://discovery.nationalarchives.gov.uk/find-an-archive

The Gazette
UK's official public record, comprised of three publications: the *London Gazette*, *Belfast Gazette* and *Edinburgh Gazette*.
www.thegazette.co.uk

BIBLIOGRAPHY

Barty-King, Hugh. *The worst poverty: a history of debt and debtors* (Sutton Publishing Ltd, 1991)

Bates, Denise. *Historical Research Using British Newspapers* (Pen & Sword, 2016)

Bevan, Amanda. *Tracing your ancestors in The National Archives: the website and beyond*, (7th edition, The National Archives, 2006)

Brown, Roger Lee. *A History of the Fleet Prison, London: the anatomy of the Fleet* (Edwin Mellen Press Ltd, 1996)

Brown, Professor William. *The Fleet: a brief account of the ancient prison called the Fleet in the City of London* (1843)

Buckley, W. *The Jurisdiction and Practice of the Marshalsea & Palace Courts, with Tables of Costs and Charges, and an Appendix Containing Statutes, Letters Patents, Rules of Court, &c. &c.* (1827)

Byrne, Richard. *Prisons and Punishments of London* (Harrap Books Ltd, 1989)

Calland, Gary. *A History of the Devon County Prison for Debtors in St. Thomas* Little History Publications, 1999)

Cohen, Jay. 'The History of Imprisonment for Debt and its Relations to the Development of Discharge in Bankruptcy' in *The Journal of Legal History*, vol.3 (Frank Cass, 1982)

Dixon, W. Hepworth. *The London Prisons: with an account of the more distinguished persons who have been confined in them. To which is added, a description of the chief provincial prisons* (Jackson & Welford, 1850)

Finn, Margot C. *The character of credit: personal debt in English culture, 1740–1914* (Cambridge University Press, 2003)

Fowler, Simon & Ruth Paley. *Family Skeletons* (The National Archives, 2005)

Gibson, Jeremy and Jeremy Brett. *Local Newspapers 1750–1920* (3rd Edition, Family History Partnership, 2011)

Grant, James. *Sketches of London* (W.S. Orr & Co, 1838)

Howard, John. *The State of the Prisons in England and Wales with Preliminary Observations and an Account of Some Foreign Prisons* (Warrington, 1772)

Gratzer, Karl and Dieter Stiefeld (eds). *History of Insolvency and Bankruptcy from an International Perspective* (Södertörns högskola, 2008)

Howard, John. *Appendix to the State of the Prisons in England and Wales &c. Containing a Farther Account of Foreign Prisons and Hospitals, with Additional Remarks on the Prisons of this Country* (Warrington, 1780)

Howse, Geoffrey. *A History of London's Prisons* (Wharncliffe Books, 2012)

Jenkins, Peter R. (Ed.). *And Bankruptcy Ensues: a Victorian lexicon of finance, compiled from the 'Dictionary of Trade, Commerce and Navigation (1844)* (Dragonwheel Books, 1996)

Lester, V. Markham. *Victorian Insolvency: bankruptcy, imprisonment for debt, and company winding-up in nineteenth-century England* (Clarendon Press, 1995)

Marriner, Sheila. 'English bankruptcy Records and Statistics before 1850' in *Economic History Review*, Vol.33 D series (1980)

Marston, Edward. *Prison: five hundred years of life behind bars*. The National Archives, 2009)

Mayhew, Henry & John Binny. *The Criminal Prisons of London and Scenes of Prison Life* (Griffin, Bohn & Co.,1862)

McConville, Sean. *A History of English Prison Administration, Volume I 1750–1877*. (Routledge & Kegan Paul, 1981)

Moore, Susan T. *Tracing Your Ancestors through the Equity Courts: a guide for family and local historians* (Pen & Sword, 2017)

Neild, James. *An Account of the Rise, Progress, and Present State of the Society for the Discharge and Relief of Persons Imprisoned for Small Debts Throughout England and Wales* (Nichols & Son, 1802)

Bibliography

Ribin, Gerry R. *Debtors, Creditors and the County Courts, 1846–1914: some source material* (Frank Cass, 1996)

Sheehan, Wayne Joseph. *The London Prison System 1666–1795* (unpublished thesis, 1975)

Vaughan, Sir Ronald Lomax. *The law and practice in bankruptcy.* (First published 1886. Numerous later updated editions.)

Wetherfield, G. Manley. *A Manuel of Bankruptcy and Imprisonment for Debt under the Bankruptcy and Debtors Act 1869* (Longmans, 1869)

White, Jerry. *Mansions of Misery: a biography of the Marshalsea Debtors' Prison.* (The Bodley Head, 2016)

London Metropolitan Archives Information Leaflets
  A Brief Guide to the Middlesex Sessions Records (Number 39)
  Sessions Records for the City of London and Southwark (Number 40)
  Prison Records (Number 59)
  Imprisoned Debtors (Number 66)
  The County of London Sessions (Number 67)
  The Civic Courts of the City of London (Number 68)

The National Archives Research Guides
  Bankrupts and Insolvent Debtors
  Chancery Equity Suits After 1558
  Chancery Equity Suits Before 1558
  Civil Litigants
  Court of King's Bench Records 1200–1600
  Court of Requests Records 1485–1642
  Court of Star Chamber Records 1485–1642
  Equity Proceedings in the Court of Exchequer

LIST OF ILLUSTRATIONS

'Discovery of Jingle in the Fleet' by Phiz (Hablot Knight Browne), in *Pickwick Papers* by Charles Dickens (1837) **W**

Mr Dorrit is released from debtors' prison: 'The Marshalsea becomes an orphan' by Phiz (Hablot Knight Browne), in *Little Dorrit* by Charles Dickens (1856) **W**

View of Boulogne port, by Arnoult, mid-nineteenth century **A**

'Morning and in Low Spirits – a Scene in a Lock up House' by Robert Cruickshank, in *The English Spy*, 1826 **A**

Westminster Hall, by Thomas Rowlandson in Ackermann's *The Microcosm of London* vol.2 (1809) **W**

Court of Kings Bench, by Thomas Rowlandson in Ackermann's *The Macrocosm of London*, vol.2 (1809) **W**

Circuits of the Commissioners for the Relief of Insolvent Debtors, Summer Circuits, 1847 **A**

Order for hearing the petition of James Pitt of Bodenham, Herefordshire, butcher, a prisoner in Hereford Gaol; dated 6 June 1835; pursuant to the Act for the Relief of Insolvent Debtors in England **A**

Court of Common Pleas: Plea Roll, Mary Calley v. Henry Tasker (TNA: CP 40/3460 Rot. 1784) **TNA**

Court of King's Bench: Plea Roll, Edward Hancock and William Cullock (TNA: KB 122/95) **TNA**

The Rake's Progress, plate 4, 'Arrested for Debt as Going to Court'. From the original picture by William Hogarth, engraved by H. Adlard, published by Jones & Co. **A**

A Whistling Shop. Tom and Jerry visiting Logic on board the Fleet'. Drawn and engraved by I.R. & G. Cruikshank. Published in *Life in London* by Pierce Egan (Sherwood, Jones & Co., 1821) **A**

List of Illustrations

Burning of Newgate Prison during the Gordon Riots. Published in *Old and New London* vol. 2 (Cassell, Petter & Galpin, 1878) **A**

Farringdon Street and the Fleet Prison. Published in *London and its Environs in the Nineteenth Century* (Jones & Co, London, 1829) **A**

The Begging Grate at the Fleet Street Prison, by Thomas Hosmer Shepherd, early nineteenth century **W**

Rules of the King's Bench Prison. Printed and published by W. Belch (1830) **W**

Interior of the Fleet Prison – the Racquet Court. Published in *Old and New London*, vol.2 (Cassell, Petter & Galpin, 1878) **A**

A Wedding in the Fleet: from an eighteenth-century print. Published in *Old and New London* vol.2 (Cassell, Petter & Galpin, 1878) **A**

The Last Remains of the Fleet Prison. Published in *Old and New London*, vol.2 (Cassell, Petter and Galpin, 1878) **A**

North View of the Marshalsea, Southwark before the New Buildings. Published in *Gentleman's Magazine*, May 1804 **A**

Racquet Court of the Marshalsea Prison. Published in *Old and New London* vol.6 by Cassell, Petter & Gilpin, 1878 **W**

King's Bench Prison, Principal Entrance. Published in *London and its Environs in the Nineteenth Century* (Jones & Co., London, 1829) **A**

Interior of the King's Bench Prison. Drawn by J.C. Whichelo and engraved by T.L. Busby. Published by G. Smeeton, 1812 **A**

Plaque, commemorating 'Nell Gwynne's bounty', on the site of Whitecross Street Prison **A**

Surrey County Gaol, Horsemonger Lane, early nineteenth century **A**

Fleet Prison Commitment Book, June 1812–September 1813 (TNA: PRIS 1/27) **TNA**

Marshalsea Prison Commitment and Discharge Registers: entries for John Dickens (Dickins) on 20 February (TNA: PRIS 11/7) **TNA**

Names of prisoners in custody of Sheriffs in Debtors 'Prison,

215

September 1817 (LMA: CLA/034/01/008) **LMA**
Sheriffs' Court Roll (LMA: CLA/025/CT/01/103) **LMA**
Interior of the Ancient Chapel of St Mary Magdalen, Guildhall: Now the Court of Requests. Published by Robert Wilkinson, October 1817 **W**
'Alsatia' (Whitefriars). Based on Agas map (published 1633)**A**
Approximate area covered by the Liberty of the Mint, Southwark. Based on 1720 map **A**
London Gazette, 11 June 1723, Issue 6172
The Poultry Compter (published in *London Old & New* vol.1) **W**
Wood Street Compter: Petition for charity (LMA: CLA/040/08/008) **LMA**
Giltspur Street Compter, 1840 (published in *London Old & New*, vol.2') **A**
Southwark Compter: Committals for Debt 1818 (LMA: CLA/031/01/001) **LMA**
Debtors Schedule, 25 November 1773 relating to Thomas Gard, a fugitive returned from Brussels (LMA: CLA/047/LJ/17/061) **LMA**
Debtors' Appearance Book (SHC: QS3/2/7) **SHC**
Find-an-archive screenshot
Catalogue entry for Pleas in the Wiltshire County Court
Petition from the creditors of Edward Reeves to the Wiltshire Quarter Sessions, 1748 (W&SHC: A1/120) **W&S**
Prisoners held for debt etc. in Fisherton Anger Gaol on 1 January 1748 (W&SHC: A1/120) **W&S**
Extract from 'Guide to archives and other collections of documents relating to Surrey: Quarter Sessions with other records of the Justices of the Peace' (Surrey Record Society, Number XXXII, 1931) **A**
Example of document from the Case Book for William Blake of Tooting in the County of Surrey who owed Elizabeth Pack £103.0.0, 22 October 1830 (TNA: B 3/678) **TNA**
Oscar Wilde **W**
Gentleman's Magazine vol.56 (1786)

List of Illustrations

List of persons declared Bankrupts, published in *The London Magazine or Gentleman's Monthly Intelligencer*, October 1732
The Jurist, No 586, Vol.XII, 1 April 1848 **A**
A List of Bankrupts from December 24, 1811, to June 19, 1812, published in 'The European Magazine & London Review', vol.61 (January-June1812)
Stamford Mercury, 28 November 1717
Bankruptcies & Liquidations, listed in the *City of London Directory*, 1877

A: Author's collection
LMA: Reproduced by permission of London Metropolitan Archives
SHC: Reproduced by permission of Surrey History Centre
TNA: Reproduced by permission of The National Archives
W: Wikimedia Commons
W&S: Reproduced by permission of Wiltshire & Swindon History Centre

INDEX

Page numbers in **bold** indicate main entry(ies)

Acts
  1285 Statute of Merchants, x
  1377 & 1379 Conformation of liberties etc Acts, 125
  1542 Statute of Bankrupts, 165
  1571 Bankrupts Act of, 167
  1694 and 1695 Marriage Duty Acts, 77
  1723 The Mint in Southwark Act 125
  1724 Insolvent Debtors Relief Act, 131
  1774 Health of Prisons Act, 63
  1815 Gaol Fees Abolition Act, xii, 42, 58, 63, 65, 68, 86,
  1823 Gaols etc. (England) Act, xii
  1825 Bankrupts (England) Act, 166, 171
  1835 Prisons Act, xiii
  1842 Insolvent Debtors Act, xi
  1844 Arrangement Between Debtors and Creditors Act, 3
  1849 County Courts Act, 19
  1861 Bankruptcy Act, xi
  1862 Queen's Prison Discontinuance Act, 86
  1869 Bankruptcy Act, 172
  1869 Debtors' Act of, 64
  1873 & 1875 Supreme Court of Judicature Acts, 17
All the Year Round (Charles Dickens), 2, 80
Alsatia, 125
Appeals, Bankruptcy, **182**
Assize Courts, 13, **19-20**

Ballatine, Sergeant, 5
Bankrupt Directory, Being a Complete Register of All the Bankrupts, with their Residences, Trades & Dates When They Appeared In The London Gazette, From December 1820 To April 1843, 195
Bankruptcy Appeals, **182**
Bankruptcy Case Files, **173-177**
Bankruptcy Court, xi, 28, 171
Bankruptcy, District Court, xi
Bankruptcy Functions of the Board of Trade, 28, 172, **183-185**
Bankruptcy Proceedings before 1869, **177-180**
Bankruptcy Proceedings from 1869, **180-182**

Index

Bankrupts in England and Wales in the Year 1861, 196
Bankrupts in England, Scotland and Wales in the Year 1851, 196
Bankrupts' Register, 197
Bartholomew Fair, 76
Bedford, xi, xii, 63
Begging Grate, 73, 74
Belle Sauvage Public House, 76
Birmingham Court of Requests, 154
Birmingham Debtors' Prison, 153, 154
Board of Trade, 28, 172, **183-185**
Boulogne, 4, 5
Brideshead Revisited (Evelyn Waugh), 166
British Newspaper Archive, 189, 194
Brougham, Henry, 152
Burdon's Hotel, 89
Burney Collection, 193

Calais, 4, 5
Case Files, Bankruptcy, **173-177**
Census Returns, **111-112**
Certificate of Conformity, 169, 170, 171
Chancery Court, 10, 12, **18**, 65, 74, 171, 173
Charity, **23-24**, 60, 128, 130
Chummed, Chumming, 67
City of London Court of Requests, 10, 87, **120-121**

City of London Courts, **114-121**
City of London Directory, 195
Civil Litigants, 213
Clandestine Marriage, 77-80
Coldbath Fields Prison, xi
Common Law Courts, 12, **13-15**, 18, 20, 30, **32-48**
Compters, *see* London Compters
County Debtors, **153**
County Courts, **124-125, 153**
Court of Requests, **152-153**
  Dorset, **161-162**
  Prisons, **153-154**
  Reports of Inspectors of Prisons, **154-157**
  Surrey, **162-164**
  Trial, **152**
  Wiltshire, **157-161**
Court for the Relief of Insolvent Debtors, x, xi, **25-29**, 188
Court of Common Pleas, 10, 12, 13, **15**, 17, 18, **32-39**, 72, 162, 166, 167, 173
Court of Exchequer, 10, 12, 13, 17, **17-18**, **44-48**, 72, 162, 173
Court of Husting, 114
Court of King's (Queen's) Bench, 10, 12, 13, **16-17**, 65, 162, 166, 167, 173
Court of Requests for the City of London, 10, 87, 121, **123-124**
Court of Requests 13, **18-19**, **49-51**

219

Courts of Requests, (local) 13, **121-124**, 150, **152-153**, 153
Courts of Requests (London), 87, 90, 114, **138, 152**
Court of Star Chamber, 13, **19, 51-52**, 72
Courts (general), **12-13**
Court of Bankruptcy, xi, 13, 18, 20, 25, 28, **171-172**, 184, 196
Credit Drapers' Gazette, 6
Cripplegate Coffeehouse, 89
Cry of the Oppressed (Moses Pitt), 1
Curia Regis, *see* Court of King's (Queen's) Bench

David Copperfield (Charles Dickens), ix, 25, 80
Debtors in London With List of Prisons, 1712-20, 130
Debtors Taking Sanctuary in The Mint in Southwark & Petitioners List, 130
Defoe, Daniel, 127, 129, 169
Devon County Prison for Debtors, 60
Dickens, Charles, ix, 82
Dickens, John, ix, xii, 82, 100
Directories, **195-197**
Discovery, **30-31**, 150
Dixon, William Hepworth, 59, 65
Dorset, **161-162**
Dublin Gazette, 188

Duns, 126

Ecclesiastical Courts, 10
Edinburgh Gazette, 188
Equity Courts, **18, 49-57**
European Magazine & London Review, 191
Exchequer of Pleas, *see* Court of Exchequer
Exposing Defaulters, **5-8**

Find-an-Archive, **150-151**
Fleet Marriages, **77-80**
Fleet Prison, xi, xii, 22, 23, 65-71, **72- 80**, 80, 83, 86, 92, **93-99**
Fortunes and Misfortunes of the Famous Moll Flanders (Daniel Defoe), 127
Fry, Elizabeth, xii

Gazettes, **187-188**
Gentleman's Magazine, **189-191**
Giltspur Street Compter, xi, 92, 132, **137-139**, 142, 144
Gordon Riots, **70-71**, 73, 92, 134
Gordon, Lord George, 71
Grant, James, 61, 69, 75, 83, 87
Great Fire of London, 73
Guardians or, Society for the Protection of Trade Against Swindlers and Sharpers, 6
Gurney, Joseph John, xii
Gwynne, Nell, 89, 90

Index

Habeas Corpus, Writ of, 63
Hamilton, Lady Emma, 3
Hammurabi Code, ix
Hampshire County Gaol, 156
Hardwicke's Marriage Act, 80
Hathi Trust, 190, 191
High Court of Justice in Bankruptcy, 20, 172
Horsemonger Lane Prison, 65, **90-91**, 92, **108**
Howard, John, xi, 22, 63, 68, 74, 80, 81, 92, 141

Idler, 6, 62
Inquests, **142**
Insolvent Debtors Court, 13, 25, 29
Iris Oifigiúil *see* Dublin Gazette
Isle of Man, 3

John Doe and Richard Roe, **48-49**
Joint-Stock Company, 176
Journals, **187-194**
Jurist, **191**
Justice Room (London), 114

King's (Queen's) Bench Prison, xi, xii, 4, 25, 65-71, 74, 76, 78, 80, 81 **83-86**, 157
King's Bench Court *see* Court of King's (Queen's) Bench

L'hotel Anglais, 5

Lancaster Castle, 60, 61
Leach, William, xi
Liberty of the Fleet, 69
Little Dorrit, (Charles Dickens) xii, 82
London Coffee House, 75, 76
London Compters *see* under: Giltspur Street, Poultry, Southwark, Wood Street
London Court of Bankruptcy, 20, 28, 171, 172, 173, 175
London Gazette, 130, 131, 168, 169, 171, 172, **187-188**, 189, 191, 195
London Magazine or Gentleman's Monthly Intelligencer, 191
London Prisons, 65
  see also under: Coldbath Fields, Fleet, Horsemonger Lane, King's (Queen's) Bench, Ludgate, Marshalsea, Newgate, Queen's, Whitechapel, Whitecross Street
Ludgate Prison, 69, 87, 92, **142**

Magna Carta Liberatum, ix
Manchester Guardian Society for the Protection of Trade, 6
Marshalsea Prison, xi, xii, 24, 65, 67, 68, 69, 70, **80-83**, 86, 92, 93, **99-100**, 109
Mayor's Court (London), 10, 114, **115-117**

221

Merchant of Venice (William Shakespeare), 168
Metropolitan County Courts, 172
Middlesex Court of Requests, 121
Mint, 78, 125, 126, 127, 129, 130

Newgate, Prison xii, 71, 87, **92, 108-109**
New Mint, 131
Newspapers, **187-194**
Nineteenth Century Newspapers Digital Archive, 194

Oglethorpe, James, xii
Oxford County Gaol and House of Correction, 157
Oxford Gazette, 187

Palace Court, 13, **19, 52-55,** 80
Palatinate of Lancaster Court of Common Pleas, 13, **20, 55-57,** 72
Pari Passu, 166
Peel, Robert, xiii
Periodicals, **187-194**
Perry's Gazette, **188-187**
Petitioners Against Imprisonment for Debt Listed in the 'London Gazette', 1712-24, 130
Petty Sessions, 114

Picture of Dorian Grey (Oscar Wilde), 186
Plea Rolls, 31
Posteas Files, 31
Poultry Compter, xi, 92, **132-134**
Prisoners' Inquests, **142**
Prisons, 153
  see also under: Birmingham Debtors', Coldbath Fields, Devon County, Fleet, Hampshire County, Horsemonger Lane, King's (Queen's) Bench, Ludgate, Marshalsea, Newgate, Oxford County, Queen's, Southampton, Surrey County, Whitechapel, Whitecross Street
Provincial Newspapers, **193-194**

Quarter Sessions, 10, 13, 21, 27, 29, 150, **152**
Queen's Prison, 70, 80, **83-86,** 92, 93, 101

Release of Insolvent Debtors in Middlesex, **145-146**
Release of Insolvent Debtors in Southwark, **146-149**
Release of Insolvent Debtors in the City of London, **142-145**
Reports of the Inspectors of Prisons of Great Britain, 60, **154-157**

Index

Rules of the Fleet etc, 60, 69, 74-76, 78, 81, 85

St Martin's Le Grand, 125
Sanctuary, **125-131**
Sessions of the Peace for the City of London or for Middlesex, 113
Sheriffs' Court (London), 10, 114, **117-120**
Sketches in London, 61, 69, 75, 83, 87
Society for the Protection of Trade, 6
Southampton Gaol, 3
Southwark Compter, **139-140**
Southwark County Court, 153
Southwark Court of Requests, 121, 153
Sponging House, 10
State of The Prisons in England, and an Account of the Principal Lazarettos of Europe, 63
Supreme Court of Judicature, 13, **20**, 28
Surrey County Gaol, 65, 90
Surrey, **162-164**

Tap, 67, 86
Topographical History of Surrey, 90
Tower Hamlets Court of Requests, 121, 122

Wapping, or New Mint, 131
Westminster Court of Requests, 121
Whitechapel Prison, **141**
Whitecross Street Prison, 25, 65, 69, 70, **87-90**, 92, **106-108**
Whitefriars Convent, 125
Wilde, Oscar, **185-186**
Wiltshire, **157-161**
Wood Street Compter, xi, 92, 132, **134-137**
Writ of Habeas Corpus, 63